Bill

Enjoy every endorphin!

Photo Credits

Cover photo: imago sportfotodienst GmbH
Back cover photo: © Thomas Northcut/Photodisc/Thinkstock
Photos: see individual photos
Cover design: Sabine Groten

Your Personal Running Journal

Jeff Galloway

Meyer & Meyer Sport

British Library Cataloguing in Publication Data
A catalogue record for this book is available from the British Library

Jeff Galloway
Your Personal Running Journal
Maidenhead: Meyer & Meyer Sport (UK) Ltd., 2012
ISBN 978-1-84126-340-3

© 2012 Meyer & Meyer Sport (UK) Ltd.
Aachen, Beirut, Budapest, Cairo, Cape Town, Dubai, Indianapolis,
Kindberg, Maidenhead, Sydney, Olten, Singapore, Tehran, Toronto
Member of the World
Sport Publishers' Association (WSPA)
www.w-s-p-a.org
Printed and bound by: B.O.S.S Druck und Medien GmbH, Germany
ISBN 978-1-84126-340-3
E-Mail: info@m-m-sports.com
www.m-m-sports.com

Personal Information

_____

Name

_____

Address

_____

Phone/e-mail

_____

Notes

_____

_____

_____

_____

Contents

1 Welcome to the Galloway Training Method!

By using the key elements of my program, and this journal, you can take control over your training, avoid injuries and excess fatigue, while realizing the wonderful empowerment of the training journey. The Galloway method offers a series of tools to manage your training and predict potential.

• Your current potential and realistic training pace will be suggested by the "Magic Mile"

• Your individualized run-walk-run strategy will be suggested, based upon the pace per mile. Runs with walk breaks will give you all of the endurance while reducing fatigue and injury risk. Many runners improve finish time when they shift to run-walk-run in races.

• Training Schedules in this journal will give you a training blueprint for finishing: 5K, 1OK, Half Marathon and Marathon.

• After doing several "Magic Miles" you can predict goal pace potential and a successful run-walk-run strategy to improve finish time in your race. If you are running "to finish" the MM will allow you to choose how much you want to slow down from an "all-out" effort.

• As you "pencil in" the weekend runs and the two "maintenance runs" during each week, you will set up your training plan. You can also schedule various training elements of your choice.

• By recording each run in the journal, you'll be able to analyze the data. There is usually a reason for injuries, hitting the fatigue wall, slowing down. With the right data, you can learn from mistakes—and embrace the elements of success.

• During your next training cycle, after analyzing the data, you can adjust training elements for improvement.

Enjoy every minute . . . Enjoy the endophin rush

2   Galloway Training Components

Each of the following components develops specific capabilities. By blending them, regularly, you can improve with little or no risk of injury.

Magic Mile (page 14)

This is a reality check on your goal and will help you set the right pace for the following:

• Goal setting – how much improvement is realistic

• Long run

• Speed segments, if run

• Your goal race

The long run (page 15)

This is the key element of any training program. Each long run improves endurance, pushes back the fatigue "wall," and improves performance potential.

Galloway Run-Walk-Run method (page 17)

The right insertion of strategic walk breaks will erase fatigue from the beginning of the run, speed recovery, allow you to carry on life's activities, and can significantly improve finish time.

Rest days

The breakdown that occurs when you increase speed or distance stimulates physilogical improvements – if there is strategic rest after the stress. During the rest days, repair and rebuilding occur in the muscles, tendons, cardiovascular system, mitochondria, etc.

Cadence drills (page 138)

Schedule these simple drills once or twice a week to improve running efficiency. Improving cadence can help you maintain pace at the end of races, when your stride shortens due to fatigue.

Getting faster (pages 23-24)

Only for those who have run a race and want to improve time.

- Longer long runs – better endurance improves speed

- Speed workouts – allow you to run farther at your goal pace without slowing down

- Hill sessions – best workouts to build strength and prepare for hills in a race

- Acceleration-gliders – improve your speed adaptations at top capacity and get you ready for faster running. Learning how to glide will conserve your resources

- Race rehearsal segments – one day a week, practice running at race pace, inserting walk breaks at various intervals to find which works best.

Balance

Putting all of the elements together (including rest between workouts) so that you allow the body to recover, rebuild and better adapt to the running motion.

3   Choosing a Motivating Goal

This journal has weekly entries for one full year. While the normal training season is 3-6 months, it helps to have projected goals beyond the current goal. The best resource book for a full year's training is A YEAR ROUND PLAN – which schedules all of the elements needed for 5K, 10K, Half Marathon and Marathon over 52 weeks. You can also use the schedules in this book (5K, 10K, 13.1 mi, Marathon) as a guide.

Most runners have several goals during a training season. The "general goals," listed below, can be included as part of an endurance goal or performance improvement program. Look over the following and pick the ones that make sense to YOU, and then look for dates of races when you want to achieve them.

General goals

- Injury free – Reduce the number of non running days due to injury, to zero.

- Burning fat—Generally possible when training for an endurance goal but not recommended when going for time goals

- Feeling good on every run—looking forward to the next run

- Running until you're 100 – this is my primary goal and the subject of my book of that title

Endurance goals

- Gradually increasing the long run to a certain distance

- Finishing a race that is longer than you usually run (no time goal)

- Your first 5K, or 10K

- Your first, 10 mile or Half Marathon

- Your first Marathon

- Time Improvement Goals

- Read the "Setting up your speed workouts" section on pages 23-24

- Choose a training book as resource see www.JeffGalloway.com

4   Picking Your Best Race

Before choosing a race . . .

Look on the website of the prospective race and find the "course closing time" (CCT). This is the slowest time allowed as an "official finisher." Look at your recent races and/or your recent "Magic Miles" (read all of the details on page 14). It's not a good idea to enter an event when your predicted finish time or recent finish times are close to or slower than CCT).

What is the enrollment? Large races are often more fun and engaging, with crowds of spectators. The downside is the weaving between runners can slow you down. Each time you zig or zag, you'll add to the distance covered. In races with over 30,000 participants, the extra distance is often a mile or more in a marathon/half a mile in a half marathon. Extra distance means a slower finish time.

What is the projected weather? Temperature has a major effect on finish time. I've surveyed this and found that most marathoners slow down 30 seconds a mile for every 5 degree increase above 60F. This means that metric/centigrade runners will slow down 20 sec per kilometer for every 2 degree temperature increase above 14C.

Sightseeing? I suggest investigating points of interest in the area: museums, national parks, etc. The Disney events, for example, offer activities for family members and reward them for enduring your absence during long runs.

Terrain, elevation change, and past participants' comments.

Visit www.marathonguide.com for lots of good information.

5   The "Magic Mile"

The "Magic Mile" time trials (MM) are reality checks on your pacing. These should be done on the weeks noted on the schedules (starting on page 149). The MM has been the best predictor of current potential and helps us set a realistic training pace. With this information, you can decide how hard to run during various situations. (If you have any injuries you should not do the MM)

- Warm up for these with about 10 minutes of very easy running with liberal walk breaks

- Do 4-6 accelerations as on page 138 – no sprinting

- Run around a track if at all possible (or a very accurately measured segment)

- Time yourself for 4 laps (1,600 meters). Start the watch at the beginning, and keep it running until you cross the finish of the 4th lap. Note this time in your journal.

- **On the first MM, don't run all-out: run at a pace that is slightly faster than your current 5K or 10K pace.**

- Only one MM is done on each day it is assigned

- On each successive MM (usually 3 weeks later), your mission is to beat the previous best time. Be sure to record each MM time in the journal.

- Don't ever push so much that you hurt your feet, knees, etc.

- Jog slowly for the rest of the distance assigned on that day taking as many walk breaks as you wish.

- At the end of the program we will use the fastest MM time to set a realistic pace in your race.

6 Setting the Pace for Long Runs

1. You may use current pace per mile or kilometer from a marathon, and add 2 minutes per mile or 1:30 per kilometer.

OR

2. The "Magic Mile" (MM) can also help you set this pace. During the beginning of your program, you can run the magic mile once a week. The first MM should not be run very fast – just write down your time in the journal as a reference. Follow the instructions in the MM section, above. Use the MMs on the schedules at the end of the program to set a realistic goal for the race itself.

3. Take your fastest time of the three and multiply by 1.3. This will tell you current potential per mile in a marathon if everything was perfect.

4. Add two more minutes to this potential time for a safe long run pace.

5. Add 30 sec/mi for every 5F degrees above 60F. Centigrade/metric runners should add 20 sec per kilometer for every 2C above 14C.

Remember to convert minutes and seconds into minutes and hundredths of a minute

Example: 10:15 MM time for 1,600 meters:

> 10.25 X 1.3 = 13.325 minutes or 13:20 per mile in minutes and seconds
>
> Then, add two minutes to slow down the pace for long runs
>
> 13:20 + 2:00 = 15:20 per mile pace at 60F/14C

To convert per mile pace to per kilometer pace, convert the mile time into minutes and hundredths of a minute and multiply by .62 (Example: 10 min/mi = 6.2 min/km or 6:12 per kilometer.

To convert a per kilometer pace to a per mile pace, multiply the kilometer pace by 1.613

> Example: 6:12 per kilometer = 6.2 min/km X 1.613 = 10.00 min or 10:00 min/mi

Pace for other runs. If you have a time goal, follow the instructions on page 23. Those who are running for enjoyment or "to finish" their current goal race, can run any speed they wish on "maintenance" days, if the body is recovering.

7 The Galloway Run-Walk-Run Method

"The scheduled use of walk breaks, gives each runner control over fatigue and running enjoyment."

One of the wonderful aspects of running is that you are the captain of your running ship. There is no definition of a "runner" that you must live up to. There are also no rules that you must follow as you do your daily run. You determine how far, how fast, how much you will run, walk, etc. While you will hear many opinions on this, running has always been a freestyle type of activity where each individual is empowered to mix and match the many variables and come out with the running experience that he or she chooses. Walk breaks are the most important component for the first time runner, and can even give the veteran a chance to improve time. Here's how it works:

Walk before you get tired

Most of us, even when untrained, can walk for several miles before fatigue sets in, because walking is an extremely efficient activity that we are bio-engineered to do for hours. Running is more work, because you have to lift your body off the ground and then absorb the shock of the landing, over and over. This is why the continuous use of the running muscles will produce fatigue, aches and pains much more quickly. If you insert a walk break into a run before your running muscles start to get tired, you allow the muscle to recover quickly during the walk. This increases your capacity for exercise, extending your endurance, while reducing the chance of soreness later that day or the next day.

The "method" concept means that you have a strategy. By using a ratio of running and walking, listed below, you will manage your fatigue. When your walk early and often from the beginning, you'll save energy resources, significantly reduce fatigue buildup, and bestow the mental confidence to cope with any challenges that may come later. Even when you don't need the extra muscle stamina and resiliency bestowed by the method, you will feel better during and after your run, and finish knowing that you could have gone further.

Beginning Runners: Insert short segments of running into a walk every minute to let the feet, muscles, joints, etc. adapt to running, without getting overwhelmed. As you

YOUR PERSONAL RUNNING JOURNAL

improve your running ability, you will reach a point where you can set the ratio of running and walking – for that day. See the GETTING STARTED book which has a 6 month entry level program.

Those who are currently running two miles or more without problems can use the table below as a guideline for the ratio of running to walking. It is always OK to insert more walking – especially in the beginning of a run.

Veteran runners tell me, almost every day, that using the correct walk break strategy allowed them to set personal records, qualify for Boston, etc., while enjoying the race experience.

"The run-walk-run method is very simple: You run for a short segment and then take a walk break, and keep repeating this pattern."

Walk breaks . . .

- Erase fatigue

- Give you control over aches, pains and injury risk

- Push back your tiredness "wall"

- Allow for endorphins to collect during each walk break – you feel good!

- Break up the distance into manageable units. ("one more minute until a walk break")

- Speed recovery

- Allow you to feel good afterward – doing what you need to do without debilitating fatigue

- Give you all of the endurance of the distance of each session – without the pain

- Allow older or heavier runners to recover fast, and feel as good or better than the younger/ligher days

© Jupiterimages/ Comstock/ Thinkstock

A short and gentle walking stride

Prime reason for the walk break is to rest the running muscles. It's better to walk slowly, with a short stride. When walking stride is too long, there has been some irritation of the shins, hamstrings and tendons behind the knee.

No need to eliminate the walk breaks

Some beginners assume that they must work toward the day when they don't have to take any walk breaks at all. This is up to the individual, but is not recommended. Remember that you decide what strategy of run-walk-run to use. There is no rule that requires you to run any ratio of run-walk on any given day. I suggest that you adjust the ratio to how you feel.

I've run for over 50 years, and enjoy running more than ever because of walk breaks. Each run I take energizes my day. I would not be able to run almost every day if I didn't insert the walk breaks early and often. I start most runs taking a short walk break every minute.

How to keep track of the walk breaks

We now have a run-walk-run timer which can be set to beep when it's time to walk, and then beep again when it's time to start up again. Check our website www.jeffgalloway.com.

Beginner's use of walk breaks

1. Start by running for 5-10 seconds, and walking 1-2 minutes

2. If you feel good during and after the run, continue with this ratio. If not, run less until you feel good.

3. After 3-6 sessions at the ratio, add 5-10 seconds of running, maintaining the same amount of walking

4. When you can run for 30 seconds, gradually reduce the walking time to 30 seconds, every 3-6 sessions

5. When 30 seconds/30 seconds feels too easy, gradually increase the running time, 5-10 sec every 3-6 sessions

6. On any given day, when you need more walking, do it. Don't ever be afraid to drop back to make the run more fun, reducing fatigue.

Table: Recommended amounts of running and walking by pace per mile

7 min per mile	run 5 minutes, walk 20-30 seconds
8 min per mile	run 4 min/walk 30 seconds
9 min per mile	4/1 (run 4 min/walk one min)
10 min per mile	3/1
11 min per mile	2:30/1
12 min per mile	2/1
13 min per mile	1/1
14 min per mile	30 sec/30 sec
15 min per mile	20 sec run/40 sec walk
16 min per mile	15 sec run/45 sec walk
17 min per mile	10 sec run/50 sec walk
18 min per mile	5 sec run/55 sec walk

Use these strategies as a guideline and adjust so that you feel strong at the end of the run.

8 How to Set up Your Training Plan

How many days per week? I believe that running every other day can produce the same training effect and performance as running more days per week when you include the appropriate training components. In fact, research shows that those who run three days a week have the lowest injury rate. Taking 48 hours between runs can repair damage, and allow for rebuilding with adaptations for improvement. The beneficial improvement from key workouts will not be realized if the quality and quantity of the rest period is not sufficient.

More experienced runners who are not having overuse injuries or lingering fatigue can choose to run more days per week. If you are running two days in a row it's best to have the first running day be easy. If you are running three days in a row, the middle day should be very easy.

If you're experiencing aches and pains that don't seem to be healing, drop back to an every other day schedule: try to stay below the threshold of further irritation.

Decide on a date for a goal and mark the days of key workouts

1. Note the goal race on the appropriate page in the journal

2. Count back in the journal and note the dates for each page

3. Mark the dates for the long runs

4. Mark the dates of other races and adjust training accordingly

5. Mark the "maintenance run days" (most commonly on Tuesday and Thursday)

6. On the "maintenance" days, assign cadence drills, acceleration-gliders, hills, etc.

7. Use the schedules in this book or my books YEAR ROUND PLAN, HALF MARATHON, MARATHON FAQs, 5K/10K.

If your goal is "to finish" you'll find schedules in this book. If you are running a race of any distance for the first time, I suggest running at training pace for the first two-thirds of the race. Then you can choose whether or how much to speed up to the finish. If you want to improve your finish time, read on.

9 Setting up Your Speed Workouts

Only those who have run a race before should attempt a time goal in a race. I suggest using a technical training resource for the speedwork and other elements needed for specific races. Here are the recommended training books (available, autographed at www.jeffgalloway.com).

5K/10K

HALF MARATHON

GALLOWAY'S MARATHON FAQS

YEAR ROUND PLAN

Using one of the schedules in your training source, "pencil in" the speed workouts on the appropriate days in the journal.

1. If you are going to run other races, write them into the journal

2. On Tuesdays, schedule cadence drills (CD), acceleration-gliders (Acg) and race rehearsals

3. On Thursdays, schedule CDs, Acgs and hills (if you are doing them).

4. Be sure to schedule a rest day, the day before long runs, hard speed workouts, or races

Race Rehearsal Workouts (Tuesday is suggested)

If you have a time goal, a "race rehearsal" segment, once a week, can give you the chance to learn how to stay at goal pace while taking walk breaks. This is the only Galloway training component during which you will be running at race pace while taking walk breaks.

1. Practice a race warm-up as noted in the first two bullet points on page 141

2. Run on a measured course or a track. It helps to know the quarter mile marks, so a track is helpful.

3. Time yourself, running at goal pace, as you take the walk breaks projected in the race.

4. Experiment with different strategies. If you are running a three mile "race rehearsal" and plan on running 10 min/mi in your race, run the first mile using (run three min/walk 1 min), the second mile (run 90 sec/walk 30 sec) and the third mile (run 60 sec/walk 20 sec). As you do this workout, once a week, you will discover which of the strategies feels best.

5. By trying variations, you can shift gears during the race, if a current strategy is not working.

Hill Training

Running hills will improve strength for running better than any other training element I've found. Practicing good hill running form will prepare you to run better and stronger on race courses that have hills.

When: Thursday is the most common day, but other non-long-run days are OK. During a 5K or 10K speed program, Thursday is often "interval day". You may decide to run hills on another day or simply suspend hill training during the speedwork season.

How steep: start with a very easy hill (1-3 %). If you will be running hills that are steeper than this in your goal race, you can move to a grade of 4-7 % after running two or more hill workouts.

How often: Even if you only do two hills, it's best to run them at least every 14 days. Once a week is even better.

- How long: Count off the number of walking steps, according to your current fitness level, marking the start and the finish. It's best to finish at the top of a hill, but this is not mandatory.

- If this is the first speed training ever: 50 steps

- If you've done sporatic speedwork: up to 100 steps

- Those who've raced once a month or more for 6 months but have not done speedwork: 150 to 200 steps

- Speedwork veterans, who have raced once a month or more for 6 months: 250-300 steps

How fast: Start at a slow pace to warmup, after about 5 steps, increase the cadence (number of steps per minute) as you go up the hill. Reduce the stride length as you go up the hill to keep the legs resiliant. You should have some huffing and puffing at the top of the hill. Don't sprint. If you have to use baby steps at the top, do so.

How much rest between each hill: Walk down the hill. Walk more if needed before doing another hill.

How many: Start with two Increase by one additional each week until you reach 8 or a number of your choice.

Uphill form: Maintain an upright body posture (forward lean not recommended), touch lightly with your feet, stay low to the ground, stride should shorten as you run up the hill – as you pick up the cadence.

Downhill form: Stay low to the ground with a light touch, don't let the stride get too long, let gravity pull you down the hill. Some call this a "fast shuffle".

10 Year at a Glance

Week #	Date	Daily	Speed sessions	Long runs	Goals
1					
2					
3					
4					
5					
6					
7					
8					
9					
10					
11					
12					
13					
14					
15					
16					
17					
18					
19					
20					
21					
22					
23					
24					
25					
26					

fn = fun   so = social   sn = scenic   sp = speed   tr = transcendental   l = long one

Week #	Date	Daily	Speed sessions	Long runs	Goals
27					
28					
29					
30					
31					
32					
33					
34					
35					
36					
37					
38					
39					
40					
41					
42					
43					
44					
45					
46					
47					
48					
49					
50					
51					
52					

11 Recording and Evaluating Your Data

This is your book

Yes, you are writing a book. You already have the outline and you have probably started recording the times and distances of your runs. As you plan workouts, according to the schedules in this journal or otherwise, your journal can document the good times, and the faster times. It will allow you to modify your plan and track the changes. Later, you can look back after success or disappointment and often find reasons for either. If we don't look back at the history of our setbacks, we will have a tendency to repeat them.

Each week:

1. Look at each workout, in advance to see if you need to make adjustments.

2. Quickly glance at the workouts you have "penciled in" over the next 8 weeks to make sure you don't have any trips, meetings, or family responsibilities that require making adjustments.

3. Each week, add another week's workouts in pencil, and note any changes in your travel, etc. schedule.

4. Each week, look back at the week before, noting problems and adjusting the schedule to move ahead.

The data recording

1. As soon as you can, after a run, write the facts in your journal. You don't have to fill in all of the spaces – but here are the important ones.

- mileage

- pace

- run-walk-run strategy

- speedwork, if done (# of repetitions-times)

- rest interval

- aches or pains – specifically where and how they hurt

- problems

2. In addition, you may also record:

- Time of run

- Total time running

- Weather

- Temp

- Precipitation

- Humidity

- Any special segments of the run (speed, hills, race, etc.)

- Running companion

- Terrain

- How did you feel (1-10)

- Comments

3. Go back over the list again and fill in more details—emotional responses, changes in energy or blood sugar level, and location of places where you had aches and pains—even if they went away during the run. You are looking for patterns of items that could indicate injury, blood sugar problems, lingering fatigue, etc.

4. Helpful additions (usually in a blank section at the bottom of the page)

- Improvement opportunities

- Things I should have done differently

- Interesting happenings:

- Funny things

- Strange things

- Stories, right brain crazy thoughts

Your morning pulse is a great guide of overstress

Recording Morning Pulse – immediately upon waking (use the graph in the back of this journal)

1. As soon as you are conscious—but before you have thought much about anything – count your pulse rate for a minute. Record it before you forget. If you don't have your journal by your bed, then keep a piece of paper handy – with a pen.

2. It is natural for there to be some fluctuations, based upon the time you wake up, how long you have been awake, etc. But after several weeks and months, these will balance themselves out. Try to catch the pulse at the instant that you are awake, before the shock of an alarm clock, thoughts of work stress, etc.

3. After two weeks or so of readings, you can establish a baseline morning pulse. Take out the top two high readings and then compute the average.

4. This will be your guide. If a morning check shows the rate to be 5% higher than your average, take an easy day. When it is 10% higher, and there is no reason for this (you woke up from an exciting dream, medication, infection, etc.) then your muscles may be tired indeed. Take the day off if you have a walk-run scheduled for that day – or walk.

5. If your pulse stays high for more than a week, call your doctor to see if there is a reason for this (medication, hormones, metabolic changes, infection, etc.). This is commonly due to overtraining or infection.

Week of Jan 1

JUST GETTING OUT THERE THREE TIMES A WEEK MEANS YOU'RE TAKI[NG] RESPONSIBILITY FOR YOUR HEALTH. WHEN YOU LEARN TO ENJOY THO[SE] THREE OUTINGS YOU'RE TAKING CHARGE OF YOUR ATTITUDE.

- Be careful with Achilles tendon.
- Build long one to 18! (must slow down in beginning).
- Slow down in the beginning of each run!

Sc = standard course; in = injury; sp = speed; l = long run; sn = scenic; tr = transcendental;
gr = group run; adj = adjustment; fn = fun; fb = fat burning; nu = nutrition
mn = mental training; ag = afterglow; so = social

Monday — Jan 1

Goal	35 min easy
Run/Walk/Run strategy used:	w/ 4-8 form accels
Time:	31 min
Distance:	@ 3 mi
AM Pulse:	52
Weather:	rainy-cold
Temp:	27°
Time:	5 AM/PM
Terrain:	rolling
Walk Break:	none

Comments
1
2 Cloudy day - dreary. Had to force
3 myself out.
4
5 * left Achilles felt tender - should have iced
6 it but didn't.
7
8 This is the year to enjoy running
9
10

Tuesday — Jan 2

Goal	45 min easy
Run/Walk/Run strategy used:	(sn)
Time:	52 min
Distance:	doesn't matter
AM Pulse:	51
Weather:	sunny-dry
Temp:	48
Time:	6 AM/PM
Terrain:	mixed
Walk Break:	—

Comments
1
2   very (t)   Sunrise!
3 one of those rare days when th[e]
4 body didn't want to... but the
5 spirit craved for transcendental
6 exertion. New trail - along river
7   Very slow + very peaceful
8 (went slow in beginning - it worked!)
9
10

Wednesday — Jan 3

Goal	off - XT
Run/Walk/Run strategy used:	run in H₂O
Time:	33 min
Distance:	—
AM Pulse:	52
Weather:	—
Temp:	—
Time:	6 AM/PM
Terrain:	
Walk Break:	

Comments
1
2 (5 sets of 10)arm running weights
3 H₂O
4
5 3 sets of 2 minutes ⎫ new
6 then 15 min easy ⎬ floted
7   ⎭ belt
8 walk for 15 min with Barb
9
10

Thursday — Jan 4

			Comments
Goal	35 min easy	1	
Run/Walk/Run strategy used:	(SC)	2	Great run with Barb, Wes +
Time:	45 min	3	Sanbo — who took out the pace
Distance:	@ 6.5	4	too fast + died at the end. The
AM Pulse:	49	5	rest of us caught up on the
Weather:	Cloudy	6	gossip. Achilles ached so I iced
Temp:	40°	7	it for 15 minutes.
Time:	6 (PM)	(8)	
Terrain:	rolling	9	
Walk Break:	—	10	

Friday — Jan 5

			Comments
Goal	45 min (sp)	1	
Run/Walk/Run strategy used:	5 × 800 meter	2	2:30 My best workout in years!
Time:	1:15	3	2:36
Distance:	7.5 mi	4	2:33 — walked 400m between each
AM Pulse:	53	(5) felt	2:37 — struggled on last one
Weather:	45°	6	
Temp:	Sunny	7 Performa	2:32
Time:	5 (PM)	(8)	2:36 Achilles ached - iced 15 min
Terrain:	track	9	12 min warm up and warm down
Walk Break:	400 m	10	

Saturday — Jan 6

			Comments
Goal	Off	1	
Run/Walk/Run strategy used:		2	Kids soccer (Mom)
Time:		3	* Westin scores goal bouncing off his back
Distance:		4	1st goal of season!
AM Pulse:	55	5	Brennan's cross country (aft)
Weather:		6	Invitational
Temp:		7	* Brennan comes from 8th to 3rd in
Time:	AM PM	8	the last half mile. I'm so proud!
Terrain:		9	
Walk Break:		10	

Sunday — Jan 7

			Comments
Goal	18 mi (1)	1	
Run/Walk/Run strategy used:	easy!	2	It was great to cover 18 miles —
Time:	2:58	3	wish I had a group
Distance:	18 mi	4	longest run in 18 months!
AM Pulse:	52	5	but...
Weather:	50°	(6)	* went too fast in the first 5 miles
Temp:	dry no wind	7	* Achilles hurt afterward - take 3 days off
Time:	7 (AM PM)	8	
Terrain:	flat	9	
Walk Break:	1 min / mi	10	

* Pulse is up — I'm not recovering — need more days off/week

Week of _____

A MARATHON BEGINS WITH A SINGLE STEP...
A LIFESTYLE CHANGE BEGINS WITH A VISION AND A SINGLE STEP.

Sc = standard course; in = injury; sp = speed; l = long run; sn = scenic; tr = transcendental; gr = group run; adj = adjustment; fn = fun; fb = fat burning; nu = nutrition
mn = mental training; ag = afterglow; so = social

Monday

Goal	1	Comments
Run/Walk/Run strategy used:	2	
Time:	3	
Distance:	4	
AM Pulse:	5	
Weather:	6	
Temp:	7	
Time: AM PM	8	
Terrain:	9	
Date Walk Break:	10	

Tuesday

Goal	1	Comments
Run/Walk/Run strategy used:	2	
Time:	3	
Distance:	4	
AM Pulse:	5	
Weather:	6	
Temp:	7	
Time: AM PM	8	
Terrain:	9	
Date Walk Break:	10	

Wednesday

Goal	1	Comments
Run/Walk/Run strategy used:	2	
Time:	3	
Distance:	4	
AM Pulse:	5	
Weather:	6	
Temp:	7	
Time: AM PM	8	
Terrain:	9	
Date Walk Break:	10	

Thursday

Goal Run/Walk/Run strategy used:	1	Comments
	2	
Time:	3	
Distance:	4	
AM Pulse:	5	
Weather:	6	
Temp:	7	
Time: AM PM	8	
Terrain:	9	
Date Walk Break:	10	

Friday

Goal Run/Walk/Run strategy used:	1	Comments
	2	
Time:	3	
Distance:	4	
AM Pulse:	5	
Weather:	6	
Temp:	7	
Time: AM PM	8	
Terrain:	9	
Date Walk Break:	10	

Saturday

Goal Run/Walk/Run strategy used:	1	Comments
	2	
Time:	3	
Distance:	4	
AM Pulse:	5	
Weather:	6	
Temp:	7	
Time: AM PM	8	
Terrain:	9	
Date Walk Break:	10	

Sunday

Goal Run/Walk/Run strategy used:	1	Comments
	2	
Time:	3	
Distance:	4	
AM Pulse:	5	
Weather:	6	
Temp:	7	
Time: AM PM	8	
Terrain:	9	
Date Walk Break:	10	

Week of _____

THE MOMENTUM OF ONE STEP LEADING TO ANOTHER IS MORE IMPORTANT THAN THE PACE.

Sc = standard course; in = injury; sp = speed; l = long run; sn = scenic; tr = transcendental; gr = group run; adj = adjustment; fn = fun; fb = fat burning; nu = nutrition
mn = mental training; ag = afterglow; so = social

Monday			Comments
Goal		1	
Run/Walk/Run strategy used:		2	
Time:		3	
Distance:		4	
AM Pulse:		5	
Weather:		6	
Temp:		7	
Time:	AM PM	8	
Terrain:		9	
Date	Walk Break:	10	

Tuesday			Comments
Goal		1	
Run/Walk/Run strategy used:		2	
Time:		3	
Distance:		4	
AM Pulse:		5	
Weather:		6	
Temp:		7	
Time:	AM PM	8	
Terrain:		9	
Date	Walk Break:	10	

Wednesday			Comments
Goal		1	
Run/Walk/Run strategy used:		2	
Time:		3	
Distance:		4	
AM Pulse:		5	
Weather:		6	
Temp:		7	
Time:	AM PM	8	
Terrain:		9	
Date	Walk Break:	10	

Week of _____

THE MOMENTUM OF ONE STEP LEADING TO ANOTHER IS MORE IMPORTANT THAN THE PACE.

Sc = standard course; in = injury; sp = speed; l = long run; sn = scenic; tr = transcendental; gr = group run; adj = adjustment; fn = fun; fb = fat burning; nu = nutrition
mn = mental training; ag = afterglow; so = social

Monday

			Comments
Goal		1	
Run/Walk/Run strategy used:		2	
Time:		3	
Distance:		4	
AM Pulse:		5	
Weather:		6	
Temp:		7	
Time:	AM PM	8	
Terrain:		9	
Date	Walk Break:	10	

Tuesday

			Comments
Goal		1	
Run/Walk/Run strategy used:		2	
Time:		3	
Distance:		4	
AM Pulse:		5	
Weather:		6	
Temp:		7	
Time:	AM PM	8	
Terrain:		9	
Date	Walk Break:	10	

Wednesday

			Comments
Goal		1	
Run/Walk/Run strategy used:		2	
Time:		3	
Distance:		4	
AM Pulse:		5	
Weather:		6	
Temp:		7	
Time:	AM PM	8	
Terrain:		9	
Date	Walk Break:	10	

Thursday	Goal	1	Comments
	Run/Walk/Run strategy used:	2	
	Time:	3	
	Distance:	4	
	AM Pulse:	5	
	Weather:	6	
	Temp:	7	
	Time: ᴬᴹ ᴾᴹ	8	
	Terrain:	9	
Date	Walk Break:	10	

Friday	Goal	1	Comments
	Run/Walk/Run strategy used:	2	
	Time:	3	
	Distance:	4	
	AM Pulse:	5	
	Weather:	6	
	Temp:	7	
	Time: ᴬᴹ ᴾᴹ	8	
	Terrain:	9	
Date	Walk Break:	10	

Saturday	Goal	1	Comments
	Run/Walk/Run strategy used:	2	
	Time:	3	
	Distance:	4	
	AM Pulse:	5	
	Weather:	6	
	Temp:	7	
	Time: ᴬᴹ ᴾᴹ	8	
	Terrain:	9	
Date	Walk Break:	10	

Sunday	Goal	1	Comments
	Run/Walk/Run strategy used:	2	
	Time:	3	
	Distance:	4	
	AM Pulse:	5	
	Weather:	6	
	Temp:	7	
	Time: ᴬᴹ ᴾᴹ	8	
	Terrain:	9	
Date	Walk Break:	10	

Thursday

Goal	1	Comments
Run/Walk/Run strategy used:	2	
Time:	3	
Distance:	4	
AM Pulse:	5	
Weather:	6	
Temp:	7	
Time: AM PM	8	
Terrain:	9	
Date Walk Break:	10	

Friday

Goal	1	Comments
Run/Walk/Run strategy used:	2	
Time:	3	
Distance:	4	
AM Pulse:	5	
Weather:	6	
Temp:	7	
Time: AM PM	8	
Terrain:	9	
Date Walk Break:	10	

Saturday

Goal	1	Comments
Run/Walk/Run strategy used:	2	
Time:	3	
Distance:	4	
AM Pulse:	5	
Weather:	6	
Temp:	7	
Time: AM PM	8	
Terrain:	9	
Date Walk Break:	10	

Sunday

Goal	1	Comments
Run/Walk/Run strategy used:	2	
Time:	3	
Distance:	4	
AM Pulse:	5	
Weather:	6	
Temp:	7	
Time: AM PM	8	
Terrain:	9	
Date Walk Break:	10	

Week of _____

WHEN YOU BUILD A BALANCE OF PHYSICAL ENERGY, MENTAL FOCUS AND INSPIRATION YOU CAN OVERCOME ANYTHING THAT IS REALISTICALLY POSSIBLE . . . AND MANY OTHER THINGS WHICH MAY NOT SEEM POSSIBL

Sc = standard course; in = injury; sp = speed; l = long run; sn = scenic; tr = transcendental; gr = group run; adj = adjustment; fn = fun; fb = fat burning; nu = nutrition
mn = mental training; ag = afterglow; so = social

Monday

Goal	1	Comments
Run/Walk/Run strategy used:	2	
Time:	3	
Distance:	4	
AM Pulse:	5	
Weather:	6	
Temp:	7	
Time: AM PM	8	
Terrain:	9	
Date · Walk Break:	10	

Tuesday

Goal	1	Comments
Run/Walk/Run strategy used:	2	
Time:	3	
Distance:	4	
AM Pulse:	5	
Weather:	6	
Temp:	7	
Time: AM PM	8	
Terrain:	9	
Date · Walk Break:	10	

Wednesday

Goal	1	Comments
Run/Walk/Run strategy used:	2	
Time:	3	
Distance:	4	
AM Pulse:	5	
Weather:	6	
Temp:	7	
Time: AM PM	8	
Terrain:	9	
Date · Walk Break:	10	

Thursday

Goal	1	Comments
Run/Walk/Run strategy used:	2	
Time:	3	
Distance:	4	
AM Pulse:	5	
Weather:	6	
Temp:	7	
Time: AM PM	8	
Terrain:	9	
Date Walk Break:	10	

Friday

Goal	1	Comments
Run/Walk/Run strategy used:	2	
Time:	3	
Distance:	4	
AM Pulse:	5	
Weather:	6	
Temp:	7	
Time: AM PM	8	
Terrain:	9	
Date Walk Break:	10	

Saturday

Goal	1	Comments
Run/Walk/Run strategy used:	2	
Time:	3	
Distance:	4	
AM Pulse:	5	
Weather:	6	
Temp:	7	
Time: AM PM	8	
Terrain:	9	
Date Walk Break:	10	

Sunday

Goal	1	Comments
Run/Walk/Run strategy used:	2	
Time:	3	
Distance:	4	
AM Pulse:	5	
Weather:	6	
Temp:	7	
Time: AM PM	8	
Terrain:	9	
Date Walk Break:	10	

Week of _____

BY EXERCISING THREE TIMES A WEEK, YOU ESTABLISH A PROCESS WHICH WILL BESTOW MORE BENEFITS THAN YOU WILL BE ABLE TO LIST.

Sc = standard course; in = injury; sp = speed; l = long run; sn = scenic; tr = transcendental; gr = group run; adj = adjustment; fn = fun; fb = fat burning; nu = nutrition mn = mental training; ag = afterglow; so = social

Monday

Goal	1	Comments
Run/Walk/Run strategy used:	2	
Time:	3	
Distance:	4	
AM Pulse:	5	
Weather:	6	
Temp:	7	
Time: AM PM	8	
Terrain:	9	
Date Walk Break:	10	

Tuesday

Goal	1	Comments
Run/Walk/Run strategy used:	2	
Time:	3	
Distance:	4	
AM Pulse:	5	
Weather:	6	
Temp:	7	
Time: AM PM	8	
Terrain:	9	
Date Walk Break:	10	

Wednesday

Goal	1	Comments
Run/Walk/Run strategy used:	2	
Time:	3	
Distance:	4	
AM Pulse:	5	
Weather:	6	
Temp:	7	
Time: AM PM	8	
Terrain:	9	
Date Walk Break:	10	

Thursday

Goal	1	Comments
Run/Walk/Run strategy used:	2	
Time:	3	
Distance:	4	
AM Pulse:	5	
Weather:	6	
Temp:	7	
Time: AM PM	8	
Terrain:	9	
Date Walk Break:	10	

Friday

Goal	1	Comments
Run/Walk/Run strategy used:	2	
Time:	3	
Distance:	4	
AM Pulse:	5	
Weather:	6	
Temp:	7	
Time: AM PM	8	
Terrain:	9	
Date Walk Break:	10	

Saturday

Goal	1	Comments
Run/Walk/Run strategy used:	2	
Time:	3	
Distance:	4	
AM Pulse:	5	
Weather:	6	
Temp:	7	
Time: AM PM	8	
Terrain:	9	
Date Walk Break:	10	

Sunday

Goal	1	Comments
Run/Walk/Run strategy used:	2	
Time:	3	
Distance:	4	
AM Pulse:	5	
Weather:	6	
Temp:	7	
Time: AM PM	8	
Terrain:	9	
Date Walk Break:	10	

Week of _____

THE INSPIRATION FOR TODAY'S RUN IS WITHIN YOU.

Sc = standard course; in = injury; sp = speed; I = long run; sn = scenic; tr = transcendental; gr = group run; adj = adjustment; fn = fun; fb = fat burning; nu = nutrition
mn = mental training; ag = afterglow; so = social

Monday

Goal		1	Comments
Run/Walk/Run strategy used:		2	
Time:		3	
Distance:		4	
AM Pulse:		5	
Weather:		6	
Temp:		7	
Time:	AM PM	8	
Terrain:		9	
Date	Walk Break:	10	

Tuesday

Goal		1	Comments
Run/Walk/Run strategy used:		2	
Time:		3	
Distance:		4	
AM Pulse:		5	
Weather:		6	
Temp:		7	
Time:	AM PM	8	
Terrain:		9	
Date	Walk Break:	10	

Wednesday

Goal		1	Comments
Run/Walk/Run strategy used:		2	
Time:		3	
Distance:		4	
AM Pulse:		5	
Weather:		6	
Temp:		7	
Time:	AM PM	8	
Terrain:		9	
Date	Walk Break:	10	

Thursday

Goal	1	Comments
Run/Walk/Run strategy used:	2	
Time:	3	
Distance:	4	
AM Pulse:	5	
Weather:	6	
Temp:	7	
Time: AM PM	8	
Terrain:	9	
Date Walk Break:	10	

Friday

Goal	1	Comments
Run/Walk/Run strategy used:	2	
Time:	3	
Distance:	4	
AM Pulse:	5	
Weather:	6	
Temp:	7	
Time: AM PM	8	
Terrain:	9	
Date Walk Break:	10	

Saturday

Goal	1	Comments
Run/Walk/Run strategy used:	2	
Time:	3	
Distance:	4	
AM Pulse:	5	
Weather:	6	
Temp:	7	
Time: AM PM	8	
Terrain:	9	
Date Walk Break:	10	

Sunday

Goal	1	Comments
Run/Walk/Run strategy used:	2	
Time:	3	
Distance:	4	
AM Pulse:	5	
Weather:	6	
Temp:	7	
Time: AM PM	8	
Terrain:	9	
Date Walk Break:	10	

Week of _____

DON'T EVER UNDERESTIMATE THE INSPIRATIONAL VALUE
OF AN ENERGY BAR AND A CUP OF COFFEE.

Sc = standard course; in = injury; sp = speed; l = long run; sn = scenic; tr = transcendental;
gr = group run; adj = adjustment; fn = fun; fb = fat burning; nu = nutrition
mn = mental training; ag = afterglow; so = social

Monday

Goal	1	Comments
Run/Walk/Run strategy used:	2	
Time:	3	
Distance:	4	
AM Pulse:	5	
Weather:	6	
Temp:	7	
Time: AM PM	8	
Terrain:	9	
Date Walk Break:	10	

Tuesday

Goal	1	Comments
Run/Walk/Run strategy used:	2	
Time:	3	
Distance:	4	
AM Pulse:	5	
Weather:	6	
Temp:	7	
Time: AM PM	8	
Terrain:	9	
Date Walk Break:	10	

Wednesday

Goal	1	Comments
Run/Walk/Run strategy used:	2	
Time:	3	
Distance:	4	
AM Pulse:	5	
Weather:	6	
Temp:	7	
Time: AM PM	8	
Terrain:	9	
Date Walk Break:	10	

Thursday

Goal	1	Comments
Run/Walk/Run strategy used:	2	
Time:	3	
Distance:	4	
AM Pulse:	5	
Weather:	6	
Temp:	7	
Time: AM PM	8	
Terrain:	9	
Date Walk Break:	10	

Friday

Goal	1	Comments
Run/Walk/Run strategy used:	2	
Time:	3	
Distance:	4	
AM Pulse:	5	
Weather:	6	
Temp:	7	
Time: AM PM	8	
Terrain:	9	
Date Walk Break:	10	

Saturday

Goal	1	Comments
Run/Walk/Run strategy used:	2	
Time:	3	
Distance:	4	
AM Pulse:	5	
Weather:	6	
Temp:	7	
Time: AM PM	8	
Terrain:	9	
Date Walk Break:	10	

Sunday

Goal	1	Comments
Run/Walk/Run strategy used:	2	
Time:	3	
Distance:	4	
AM Pulse:	5	
Weather:	6	
Temp:	7	
Time: AM PM	8	
Terrain:	9	
Date Walk Break:	10	

Week of _____

A BODY ON THE COUCH WANTS TO REMAIN ON THE COUCH, BUT AS SOON AS YOU GET THAT BODY IN THE RUNNING MOTION IT WANTS TO KEEP RUNNING.

Sc = standard course; in = injury; sp = speed; l = long run; sn = scenic; tr = transcendental; gr = group run; adj = adjustment; fn = fun; fb = fat burning; nu = nutrition
mn = mental training; ag = afterglow; so = social

Monday

Goal	1	Comments
Run/Walk/Run strategy used:	2	
Time:	3	
Distance:	4	
AM Pulse:	5	
Weather:	6	
Temp:	7	
Time: AM PM	8	
Terrain:	9	
Walk Break:	10	

Date

Tuesday

Goal	1	Comments
Run/Walk/Run strategy used:	2	
Time:	3	
Distance:	4	
AM Pulse:	5	
Weather:	6	
Temp:	7	
Time: AM PM	8	
Terrain:	9	
Walk Break:	10	

Date

Wednesday

Goal	1	Comments
Run/Walk/Run strategy used:	2	
Time:	3	
Distance:	4	
AM Pulse:	5	
Weather:	6	
Temp:	7	
Time: AM PM	8	
Terrain:	9	
Walk Break:	10	

Date

Thursday

Goal	1	Comments
Run/Walk/Run strategy used:	2	
Time:	3	
Distance:	4	
AM Pulse:	5	
Weather:	6	
Temp:	7	
Time: AM PM	8	
Terrain:	9	
Date	Walk Break:	10	

Friday

Goal	1	Comments
Run/Walk/Run strategy used:	2	
Time:	3	
Distance:	4	
AM Pulse:	5	
Weather:	6	
Temp:	7	
Time: AM PM	8	
Terrain:	9	
Date	Walk Break:	10	

Saturday

Goal	1	Comments
Run/Walk/Run strategy used:	2	
Time:	3	
Distance:	4	
AM Pulse:	5	
Weather:	6	
Temp:	7	
Time: AM PM	8	
Terrain:	9	
Date	Walk Break:	10	

Sunday

Goal	1	Comments
Run/Walk/Run strategy used:	2	
Time:	3	
Distance:	4	
AM Pulse:	5	
Weather:	6	
Temp:	7	
Time: AM PM	8	
Terrain:	9	
Date	Walk Break:	10	

Week of _____

SPEED IS MOSTLY FOR THE EGO . . .
BUT THERE'S NOTHING WRONG WITH A WEEKLY EGO BOOST.

Sc = standard course; in = injury; sp = speed; l = long run; sn = scenic; tr = transcendental;
gr = group run; adj = adjustment; fn = fun; fb = fat burning; nu = nutrition
mn = mental training; ag = afterglow; so = social

Monday

Goal	1	Comments
Run/Walk/Run strategy used:	2	
Time:	3	
Distance:	4	
AM Pulse:	5	
Weather:	6	
Temp:	7	
Time: AM PM	8	
Terrain:	9	
Date Walk Break:	10	

Tuesday

Goal	1	Comments
Run/Walk/Run strategy used:	2	
Time:	3	
Distance:	4	
AM Pulse:	5	
Weather:	6	
Temp:	7	
Time: AM PM	8	
Terrain:	9	
Date Walk Break:	10	

Wednesday

Goal	1	Comments
Run/Walk/Run strategy used:	2	
Time:	3	
Distance:	4	
AM Pulse:	5	
Weather:	6	
Temp:	7	
Time: AM PM	8	
Terrain:	9	
Date Walk Break:	10	

Thursday

			Comments
Goal		1	
Run/Walk/Run strategy used:		2	
Time:		3	
Distance:		4	
AM Pulse:		5	
Weather:		6	
Temp:		7	
Time:	AM PM	8	
Terrain:		9	
Date	Walk Break:	10	

Friday

			Comments
Goal		1	
Run/Walk/Run strategy used:		2	
Time:		3	
Distance:		4	
AM Pulse:		5	
Weather:		6	
Temp:		7	
Time:	AM PM	8	
Terrain:		9	
Date	Walk Break:	10	

Saturday

			Comments
Goal		1	
Run/Walk/Run strategy used:		2	
Time:		3	
Distance:		4	
AM Pulse:		5	
Weather:		6	
Temp:		7	
Time:	AM PM	8	
Terrain:		9	
Date	Walk Break:	10	

Sunday

			Comments
Goal		1	
Run/Walk/Run strategy used:		2	
Time:		3	
Distance:		4	
AM Pulse:		5	
Weather:		6	
Temp:		7	
Time:	AM PM	8	
Terrain:		9	
Date	Walk Break:	10	

Week of _____

INSIDE YOU RIGHT NOW ARE THOUSANDS OF POCKETS OF CREATIVE THOUGHTS AND INSPIRATIONS. PUT ONE FOOT IN FRONT OF ANOTHER AND THEY'LL START OOZING OUT.

Sc = standard course; in = injury; sp = speed; I = long run; sn = scenic; tr = transcendental; gr = group run; adj = adjustment; fn = fun; fb = fat burning; nu = nutrition
mn = mental training; ag = afterglow; so = social

Monday

Goal	1	Comments
Run/Walk/Run strategy used:	2	
Time:	3	
Distance:	4	
AM Pulse:	5	
Weather:	6	
Temp:	7	
Time: AM PM	8	
Terrain:	9	
Date Walk Break:	10	

Tuesday

Goal	1	Comments
Run/Walk/Run strategy used:	2	
Time:	3	
Distance:	4	
AM Pulse:	5	
Weather:	6	
Temp:	7	
Time: AM PM	8	
Terrain:	9	
Date Walk Break:	10	

Wednesday

Goal	1	Comments
Run/Walk/Run strategy used:	2	
Time:	3	
Distance:	4	
AM Pulse:	5	
Weather:	6	
Temp:	7	
Time: AM PM	8	
Terrain:	9	
Date Walk Break:	10	

Thursday

Goal	1	Comments
Run/Walk/Run strategy used:	2	
Time:	3	
Distance:	4	
AM Pulse:	5	
Weather:	6	
Temp:	7	
Time: AM/PM	8	
Terrain:	9	
Date Walk Break:	10	

Friday

Goal	1	Comments
Run/Walk/Run strategy used:	2	
Time:	3	
Distance:	4	
AM Pulse:	5	
Weather:	6	
Temp:	7	
Time: AM/PM	8	
Terrain:	9	
Date Walk Break:	10	

Saturday

Goal	1	Comments
Run/Walk/Run strategy used:	2	
Time:	3	
Distance:	4	
AM Pulse:	5	
Weather:	6	
Temp:	7	
Time: AM/PM	8	
Terrain:	9	
Date Walk Break:	10	

Sunday

Goal	1	Comments
Run/Walk/Run strategy used:	2	
Time:	3	
Distance:	4	
AM Pulse:	5	
Weather:	6	
Temp:	7	
Time: AM/PM	8	
Terrain:	9	
Date Walk Break:	10	

Week of _____

YOU MUST PROVIDE THAT 1% MENTAL PUSH TO GET YOUR FEET MOVING – AND YOU'LL RECEIVE 99% ENERGY RETURN ON YOUR INVESTMENT.

Sc = standard course; in = injury; sp = speed; l = long run; sn = scenic; tr = transcendental; gr = group run; adj = adjustment; fn = fun; fb = fat burning; nu = nutrition mn = mental training; ag = afterglow; so = social

Monday				Comments
	Goal		1	
	Run/Walk/Run strategy used:		2	
	Time:		3	
	Distance:		4	
	AM Pulse:		5	
	Weather:		6	
	Temp:		7	
	Time:	AM PM	8	
	Terrain:		9	
Date	Walk Break:		10	

Tuesday				Comments
	Goal		1	
	Run/Walk/Run strategy used:		2	
	Time:		3	
	Distance:		4	
	AM Pulse:		5	
	Weather:		6	
	Temp:		7	
	Time:	AM PM	8	
	Terrain:		9	
Date	Walk Break:		10	

Wednesday				Comments
	Goal		1	
	Run/Walk/Run strategy used:		2	
	Time:		3	
	Distance:		4	
	AM Pulse:		5	
	Weather:		6	
	Temp:		7	
	Time:	AM PM	8	
	Terrain:		9	
Date	Walk Break:		10	

Thursday

Goal	1	Comments
Run/Walk/Run strategy used:	2	
Time:	3	
Distance:	4	
AM Pulse:	5	
Weather:	6	
Temp:	7	
Time: AM PM	8	
Terrain:	9	
Date Walk Break:	10	

Friday

Goal	1	Comments
Run/Walk/Run strategy used:	2	
Time:	3	
Distance:	4	
AM Pulse:	5	
Weather:	6	
Temp:	7	
Time: AM PM	8	
Terrain:	9	
Date Walk Break:	10	

Saturday

Goal	1	Comments
Run/Walk/Run strategy used:	2	
Time:	3	
Distance:	4	
AM Pulse:	5	
Weather:	6	
Temp:	7	
Time: AM PM	8	
Terrain:	9	
Date Walk Break:	10	

Sunday

Goal	1	Comments
Run/Walk/Run strategy used:	2	
Time:	3	
Distance:	4	
AM Pulse:	5	
Weather:	6	
Temp:	7	
Time: AM PM	8	
Terrain:	9	
Date Walk Break:	10	

Week of _____

ONCE YOU PUT A TRICKLE OF ENERGY TO GET YOURSELF RUNNING, YOU START A RIVER OF INSPIRATION WHICH CAN PULL YOU THROUGH DIFFICULTY.

Sc = standard course; in = injury; sp = speed; I = long run; sn = scenic; tr = transcendental; gr = group run; adj = adjustment; fn = fun; fb = fat burning; nu = nutrition
mn = mental training; ag = afterglow; so = social

Monday				Comments
	Goal		1	
	Run/Walk/Run strategy used:		2	
	Time:		3	
	Distance:		4	
	AM Pulse:		5	
	Weather:		6	
	Temp:		7	
	Time:	AM PM	8	
	Terrain:		9	
Date	Walk Break:		10	

Tuesday				Comments
	Goal		1	
	Run/Walk/Run strategy used:		2	
	Time:		3	
	Distance:		4	
	AM Pulse:		5	
	Weather:		6	
	Temp:		7	
	Time:	AM PM	8	
	Terrain:		9	
Date	Walk Break:		10	

Wednesday				Comments
	Goal		1	
	Run/Walk/Run strategy used:		2	
	Time:		3	
	Distance:		4	
	AM Pulse:		5	
	Weather:		6	
	Temp:		7	
	Time:	AM PM	8	
	Terrain:		9	
Date	Walk Break:		10	

Thursday

Goal	1	Comments
Run/Walk/Run strategy used:	2	
Time:	3	
Distance:	4	
AM Pulse:	5	
Weather:	6	
Temp:	7	
Time: AM PM	8	
Terrain:	9	
Date Walk Break:	10	

Friday

Goal	1	Comments
Run/Walk/Run strategy used:	2	
Time:	3	
Distance:	4	
AM Pulse:	5	
Weather:	6	
Temp:	7	
Time: AM PM	8	
Terrain:	9	
Date Walk Break:	10	

Saturday

Goal	1	Comments
Run/Walk/Run strategy used:	2	
Time:	3	
Distance:	4	
AM Pulse:	5	
Weather:	6	
Temp:	7	
Time: AM PM	8	
Terrain:	9	
Date Walk Break:	10	

Sunday

Goal	1	Comments
Run/Walk/Run strategy used:	2	
Time:	3	
Distance:	4	
AM Pulse:	5	
Weather:	6	
Temp:	7	
Time: AM PM	8	
Terrain:	9	
Date Walk Break:	10	

Week of _____

IT'S ALWAYS BEST TO START OUT SLOWLY.
BUT OCCASIONALLY IT'S OKAY TO GET OUT THERE AND KICK BUTT!

Sc = standard course; in = injury; sp = speed; l = long run; sn = scenic; tr = transcendental; gr = group run; adj = adjustment; fn = fun; fb = fat burning; nu = nutrition
mn = mental training; ag = afterglow; so = social

Monday

Goal		1	Comments
Run/Walk/Run strategy used:		2	
Time:		3	
Distance:		4	
AM Pulse:		5	
Weather:		6	
Temp:		7	
Time:	AM PM	8	
Terrain:		9	
Walk Break:		10	

Date

Tuesday

Goal		1	Comments
Run/Walk/Run strategy used:		2	
Time:		3	
Distance:		4	
AM Pulse:		5	
Weather:		6	
Temp:		7	
Time:	AM PM	8	
Terrain:		9	
Walk Break:		10	

Date

Wednesday

Goal		1	Comments
Run/Walk/Run strategy used:		2	
Time:		3	
Distance:		4	
AM Pulse:		5	
Weather:		6	
Temp:		7	
Time:	AM PM	8	
Terrain:		9	
Walk Break:		10	

Date

Thursday

Goal	1	Comments
Run/Walk/Run strategy used:	2	
Time:	3	
Distance:	4	
AM Pulse:	5	
Weather:	6	
Temp:	7	
Time: AM PM	8	
Terrain:	9	
Date Walk Break:	10	

Friday

Goal	1	Comments
Run/Walk/Run strategy used:	2	
Time:	3	
Distance:	4	
AM Pulse:	5	
Weather:	6	
Temp:	7	
Time: AM PM	8	
Terrain:	9	
Date Walk Break:	10	

Saturday

Goal	1	Comments
Run/Walk/Run strategy used:	2	
Time:	3	
Distance:	4	
AM Pulse:	5	
Weather:	6	
Temp:	7	
Time: AM PM	8	
Terrain:	9	
Date Walk Break:	10	

Sunday

Goal	1	Comments
Run/Walk/Run strategy used:	2	
Time:	3	
Distance:	4	
AM Pulse:	5	
Weather:	6	
Temp:	7	
Time: AM PM	8	
Terrain:	9	
Date Walk Break:	10	

Week of _____

EACH TIME YOU PUSH THROUGH A DISCOMFORT BARRIER YOU MAKE IT EASIER TO DO IT NEXT TIME.

Sc = standard course; in = injury; sp = speed; l = long run; sn = scenic; tr = transcendental; gr = group run; adj = adjustment; fn = fun; fb = fat burning; nu = nutrition
mn = mental training; ag = afterglow; so = social

Monday

Goal	1	Comments
Run/Walk/Run strategy used:	2	
Time:	3	
Distance:	4	
AM Pulse:	5	
Weather:	6	
Temp:	7	
Time: AM PM	8	
Terrain:	9	
Date Walk Break:	10	

Tuesday

Goal	1	Comments
Run/Walk/Run strategy used:	2	
Time:	3	
Distance:	4	
AM Pulse:	5	
Weather:	6	
Temp:	7	
Time: AM PM	8	
Terrain:	9	
Date Walk Break:	10	

Wednesday

Goal	1	Comments
Run/Walk/Run strategy used:	2	
Time:	3	
Distance:	4	
AM Pulse:	5	
Weather:	6	
Temp:	7	
Time: AM PM	8	
Terrain:	9	
Date Walk Break:	10	

Thursday

Goal	1	Comments
Run/Walk/Run strategy used:	2	
Time:	3	
Distance:	4	
AM Pulse:	5	
Weather:	6	
Temp:	7	
Time: AM PM	8	
Terrain:	9	
Date Walk Break:	10	

Friday

Goal	1	Comments
Run/Walk/Run strategy used:	2	
Time:	3	
Distance:	4	
AM Pulse:	5	
Weather:	6	
Temp:	7	
Time: AM PM	8	
Terrain:	9	
Date Walk Break:	10	

Saturday

Goal	1	Comments
Run/Walk/Run strategy used:	2	
Time:	3	
Distance:	4	
AM Pulse:	5	
Weather:	6	
Temp:	7	
Time: AM PM	8	
Terrain:	9	
Date Walk Break:	10	

Sunday

Goal	1	Comments
Run/Walk/Run strategy used:	2	
Time:	3	
Distance:	4	
AM Pulse:	5	
Weather:	6	
Temp:	7	
Time: AM PM	8	
Terrain:	9	
Date Walk Break:	10	

Week of _____

AN ATHLETE SAYS "GO" WHEN THE LEFT BRAIN SAYS "NO."

Sc = standard course; in = injury; sp = speed; l = long run; sn = scenic; tr = transcendental; gr = group run; adj = adjustment; fn = fun; fb = fat burning; nu = nutrition
mn = mental training; ag = afterglow; so = social

Monday

			Comments
Goal		1	
Run/Walk/Run strategy used:		2	
Time:		3	
Distance:		4	
AM Pulse:		5	
Weather:		6	
Temp:		7	
Time:	AM PM	8	
Terrain:		9	
Date Walk Break:		10	

Tuesday

			Comments
Goal		1	
Run/Walk/Run strategy used:		2	
Time:		3	
Distance:		4	
AM Pulse:		5	
Weather:		6	
Temp:		7	
Time:	AM PM	8	
Terrain:		9	
Date Walk Break:		10	

Wednesday

			Comments
Goal		1	
Run/Walk/Run strategy used:		2	
Time:		3	
Distance:		4	
AM Pulse:		5	
Weather:		6	
Temp:		7	
Time:	AM PM	8	
Terrain:		9	
Date Walk Break:		10	

Thursday

Goal	1	Comments
Run/Walk/Run strategy used:	2	
Time:	3	
Distance:	4	
AM Pulse:	5	
Weather:	6	
Temp:	7	
Time: AM PM	8	
Terrain:	9	
Walk Break:	10	

Date

Friday

Goal	1	Comments
Run/Walk/Run strategy used:	2	
Time:	3	
Distance:	4	
AM Pulse:	5	
Weather:	6	
Temp:	7	
Time: AM PM	8	
Terrain:	9	
Walk Break:	10	

Date

Saturday

Goal	1	Comments
Run/Walk/Run strategy used:	2	
Time:	3	
Distance:	4	
AM Pulse:	5	
Weather:	6	
Temp:	7	
Time: AM PM	8	
Terrain:	9	
Walk Break:	10	

Date

Sunday

Goal	1	Comments
Run/Walk/Run strategy used:	2	
Time:	3	
Distance:	4	
AM Pulse:	5	
Weather:	6	
Temp:	7	
Time: AM PM	8	
Terrain:	9	
Walk Break:	10	

Date

Week of _____

IF YOU START EACH RUN SLOWLY ENOUGH,
ALMOST EVERY RUN CAN LEAVE YOU FEELING INVIGORATED.

Sc = standard course; in = injury; sp = speed; l = long run; sn = scenic; tr = transcendental; gr = group run; adj = adjustment; fn = fun; fb = fat burning; nu = nutrition mn = mental training; ag = afterglow; so = social

Monday

Goal		1	Comments
Run/Walk/Run strategy used:		2	
Time:		3	
Distance:		4	
AM Pulse:		5	
Weather:		6	
Temp:		7	
Time:	AM PM	8	
Terrain:		9	
Date	Walk Break:	10	

Tuesday

Goal		1	Comments
Run/Walk/Run strategy used:		2	
Time:		3	
Distance:		4	
AM Pulse:		5	
Weather:		6	
Temp:		7	
Time:	AM PM	8	
Terrain:		9	
Date	Walk Break:	10	

Wednesday

Goal		1	Comments
Run/Walk/Run strategy used:		2	
Time:		3	
Distance:		4	
AM Pulse:		5	
Weather:		6	
Temp:		7	
Time:	AM PM	8	
Terrain:		9	
Date	Walk Break:	10	

Thursday

Goal	1	Comments
Run/Walk/Run strategy used:	2	
Time:	3	
Distance:	4	
AM Pulse:	5	
Weather:	6	
Temp:	7	
Time: AM PM	8	
Terrain:	9	
Date Walk Break:	10	

Friday

Goal	1	Comments
Run/Walk/Run strategy used:	2	
Time:	3	
Distance:	4	
AM Pulse:	5	
Weather:	6	
Temp:	7	
Time: AM PM	8	
Terrain:	9	
Date Walk Break:	10	

Saturday

Goal	1	Comments
Run/Walk/Run strategy used:	2	
Time:	3	
Distance:	4	
AM Pulse:	5	
Weather:	6	
Temp:	7	
Time: AM PM	8	
Terrain:	9	
Date Walk Break:	10	

Sunday

Goal	1	Comments
Run/Walk/Run strategy used:	2	
Time:	3	
Distance:	4	
AM Pulse:	5	
Weather:	6	
Temp:	7	
Time: AM PM	8	
Terrain:	9	
Date Walk Break:	10	

Week of _____

YOU BECOME AN ATHLETE WHEN A PHYSICAL CHALLENGE BECOMES A MENTAL CHALLENGE AND YOU KEEP GOING UNTIL YOU BREAK THROUGH IT.

Sc = standard course; in = injury; sp = speed; I = long run; sn = scenic; tr = transcendental; gr = group run; adj = adjustment; fn = fun; fb = fat burning; nu = nutrition
mn = mental training; ag = afterglow; so = social

Monday

Goal		1	Comments
Run/Walk/Run strategy used:		2	
Time:		3	
Distance:		4	
AM Pulse:		5	
Weather:		6	
Temp:		7	
Time:	AM PM	8	
Terrain:		9	
Date	Walk Break:	10	

Tuesday

Goal		1	Comments
Run/Walk/Run strategy used:		2	
Time:		3	
Distance:		4	
AM Pulse:		5	
Weather:		6	
Temp:		7	
Time:	AM PM	8	
Terrain:		9	
Date	Walk Break:	10	

Wednesday

Goal		1	Comments
Run/Walk/Run strategy used:		2	
Time:		3	
Distance:		4	
AM Pulse:		5	
Weather:		6	
Temp:		7	
Time:	AM PM	8	
Terrain:		9	
Date	Walk Break:	10	

Thursday	Goal	1	Comments
	Run/Walk/Run strategy used:	2	
	Time:	3	
	Distance:	4	
	AM Pulse:	5	
	Weather:	6	
	Temp:	7	
	Time: AM PM	8	
	Terrain:	9	
Date	Walk Break:	10	

Friday	Goal	1	Comments
	Run/Walk/Run strategy used:	2	
	Time:	3	
	Distance:	4	
	AM Pulse:	5	
	Weather:	6	
	Temp:	7	
	Time: AM PM	8	
	Terrain:	9	
Date	Walk Break:	10	

Saturday	Goal	1	Comments
	Run/Walk/Run strategy used:	2	
	Time:	3	
	Distance:	4	
	AM Pulse:	5	
	Weather:	6	
	Temp:	7	
	Time: AM PM	8	
	Terrain:	9	
Date	Walk Break:	10	

Sunday	Goal	1	Comments
	Run/Walk/Run strategy used:	2	
	Time:	3	
	Distance:	4	
	AM Pulse:	5	
	Weather:	6	
	Temp:	7	
	Time: AM PM	8	
	Terrain:	9	
Date	Walk Break:	10	

Week of _____

DON'T UNDERESTIMATE THE RELAXING POWER OF 45 MINUTES WORTH OF ENDORPHINS.

Sc = standard course; in = injury; sp = speed; l = long run; sn = scenic; tr = transcendental; gr = group run; adj = adjustment; fn = fun; fb = fat burning; nu = nutrition
mn = mental training; ag = afterglow; so = social

Monday				Comments
	Goal		1	
	Run/Walk/Run strategy used:		2	
	Time:		3	
	Distance:		4	
	AM Pulse:		5	
	Weather:		6	
	Temp:		7	
	Time:	AM PM	8	
	Terrain:		9	
Date	Walk Break:		10	

Tuesday				Comments
	Goal		1	
	Run/Walk/Run strategy used:		2	
	Time:		3	
	Distance:		4	
	AM Pulse:		5	
	Weather:		6	
	Temp:		7	
	Time:	AM PM	8	
	Terrain:		9	
Date	Walk Break:		10	

Wednesday				Comments
	Goal		1	
	Run/Walk/Run strategy used:		2	
	Time:		3	
	Distance:		4	
	AM Pulse:		5	
	Weather:		6	
	Temp:		7	
	Time:	AM PM	8	
	Terrain:		9	
Date	Walk Break:		10	

Thursday	Goal	1	Comments
	Run/Walk/Run strategy used:	2	
	Time:	3	
	Distance:	4	
	AM Pulse:	5	
	Weather:	6	
	Temp:	7	
	Time: AM PM	8	
	Terrain:	9	
Date	Walk Break:	10	

Friday	Goal	1	Comments
	Run/Walk/Run strategy used:	2	
	Time:	3	
	Distance:	4	
	AM Pulse:	5	
	Weather:	6	
	Temp:	7	
	Time: AM PM	8	
	Terrain:	9	
Date	Walk Break:	10	

Saturday	Goal	1	Comments
	Run/Walk/Run strategy used:	2	
	Time:	3	
	Distance:	4	
	AM Pulse:	5	
	Weather:	6	
	Temp:	7	
	Time: AM PM	8	
	Terrain:	9	
Date	Walk Break:	10	

Sunday	Goal	1	Comments
	Run/Walk/Run strategy used:	2	
	Time:	3	
	Distance:	4	
	AM Pulse:	5	
	Weather:	6	
	Temp:	7	
	Time: AM PM	8	
	Terrain:	9	
Date	Walk Break:	10	

Week of _____

MAKE A TINY BIT OF FUN IN EACH RUN
AND YOUR MOTIVATION WILL GROW.

Sc = standard course; in = injury; sp = speed; l = long run; sn = scenic; tr = transcendental; gr = group run; adj = adjustment; fn = fun; fb = fat burning; nu = nutrition
mn = mental training; ag = afterglow; so = social

Monday

Goal	1	Comments
Run/Walk/Run strategy used:	2	
Time:	3	
Distance:	4	
AM Pulse:	5	
Weather:	6	
Temp:	7	
Time: AM PM	8	
Terrain:	9	
Date — Walk Break:	10	

Tuesday

Goal	1	Comments
Run/Walk/Run strategy used:	2	
Time:	3	
Distance:	4	
AM Pulse:	5	
Weather:	6	
Temp:	7	
Time: AM PM	8	
Terrain:	9	
Date — Walk Break:	10	

Wednesday

Goal	1	Comments
Run/Walk/Run strategy used:	2	
Time:	3	
Distance:	4	
AM Pulse:	5	
Weather:	6	
Temp:	7	
Time: AM PM	8	
Terrain:	9	
Date — Walk Break:	10	

Thursday

Goal		1	Comments
Run/Walk/Run strategy used:		2	
Time:		3	
Distance:		4	
AM Pulse:		5	
Weather:		6	
Temp:		7	
Time:	AM PM	8	
Terrain:		9	
Date	Walk Break:	10	

Friday

Goal		1	Comments
Run/Walk/Run strategy used:		2	
Time:		3	
Distance:		4	
AM Pulse:		5	
Weather:		6	
Temp:		7	
Time:	AM PM	8	
Terrain:		9	
Date	Walk Break:	10	

Saturday

Goal		1	Comments
Run/Walk/Run strategy used:		2	
Time:		3	
Distance:		4	
AM Pulse:		5	
Weather:		6	
Temp:		7	
Time:	AM PM	8	
Terrain:		9	
Date	Walk Break:	10	

Sunday

Goal		1	Comments
Run/Walk/Run strategy used:		2	
Time:		3	
Distance:		4	
AM Pulse:		5	
Weather:		6	
Temp:		7	
Time:	AM PM	8	
Terrain:		9	
Date	Walk Break:	10	

Week of _____

THE FIRST 15 MINUTES OF EVERY RUN ARE A SHOCK TO THE SYSTEM. SLOW DOWN, GET THROUGH IT AND YOU'RE ON YOUR WAY.

Sc = standard course; in = injury; sp = speed; l = long run; sn = scenic; tr = transcendental; gr = group run; adj = adjustment; fn = fun; fb = fat burning; nu = nutrition
mn = mental training; ag = afterglow; so = social

Monday

Goal		1	Comments
Run/Walk/Run strategy used:		2	
Time:		3	
Distance:		4	
AM Pulse:		5	
Weather:		6	
Temp:		7	
Time:	AM PM	8	
Terrain:		9	
Date	Walk Break:	10	

Tuesday

Goal		1	Comments
Run/Walk/Run strategy used:		2	
Time:		3	
Distance:		4	
AM Pulse:		5	
Weather:		6	
Temp:		7	
Time:	AM PM	8	
Terrain:		9	
Date	Walk Break:	10	

Wednesday

Goal		1	Comments
Run/Walk/Run strategy used:		2	
Time:		3	
Distance:		4	
AM Pulse:		5	
Weather:		6	
Temp:		7	
Time:	AM PM	8	
Terrain:		9	
Date	Walk Break:	10	

Thursday

Goal	1	Comments
Run/Walk/Run strategy used:	2	
Time:	3	
Distance:	4	
AM Pulse:	5	
Weather:	6	
Temp:	7	
Time: AM PM	8	
Terrain:	9	
Date Walk Break:	10	

Friday

Goal	1	Comments
Run/Walk/Run strategy used:	2	
Time:	3	
Distance:	4	
AM Pulse:	5	
Weather:	6	
Temp:	7	
Time: AM PM	8	
Terrain:	9	
Date Walk Break:	10	

Saturday

Goal	1	Comments
Run/Walk/Run strategy used:	2	
Time:	3	
Distance:	4	
AM Pulse:	5	
Weather:	6	
Temp:	7	
Time: AM PM	8	
Terrain:	9	
Date Walk Break:	10	

Sunday

Goal	1	Comments
Run/Walk/Run strategy used:	2	
Time:	3	
Distance:	4	
AM Pulse:	5	
Weather:	6	
Temp:	7	
Time: AM PM	8	
Terrain:	9	
Date Walk Break:	10	

Week of _____

THE FASTER YOU RUN AT THE START,
THE GREATER THE CHANCE OF A NEGATIVE FEELING AT THE END.

Sc = standard course; in = injury; sp = speed; l = long run; sn = scenic; tr = transcendental; gr = group run; adj = adjustment; fn = fun; fb = fat burning; nu = nutrition mn = mental training; ag = afterglow; so = social

Monday

			Comments
Goal		1	
Run/Walk/Run strategy used:		2	
Time:		3	
Distance:		4	
AM Pulse:		5	
Weather:		6	
Temp:		7	
Time:	AM PM	8	
Terrain:		9	
Date	Walk Break:	10	

Tuesday

			Comments
Goal		1	
Run/Walk/Run strategy used:		2	
Time:		3	
Distance:		4	
AM Pulse:		5	
Weather:		6	
Temp:		7	
Time:	AM PM	8	
Terrain:		9	
Date	Walk Break:	10	

Wednesday

			Comments
Goal		1	
Run/Walk/Run strategy used:		2	
Time:		3	
Distance:		4	
AM Pulse:		5	
Weather:		6	
Temp:		7	
Time:	AM PM	8	
Terrain:		9	
Date	Walk Break:	10	

Thursday

Goal	1	Comments
Run/Walk/Run strategy used:	2	
Time:	3	
Distance:	4	
AM Pulse:	5	
Weather:	6	
Temp:	7	
Time: AM PM	8	
Terrain:	9	
Date Walk Break:	10	

Friday

Goal	1	Comments
Run/Walk/Run strategy used:	2	
Time:	3	
Distance:	4	
AM Pulse:	5	
Weather:	6	
Temp:	7	
Time: AM PM	8	
Terrain:	9	
Date Walk Break:	10	

Saturday

Goal	1	Comments
Run/Walk/Run strategy used:	2	
Time:	3	
Distance:	4	
AM Pulse:	5	
Weather:	6	
Temp:	7	
Time: AM PM	8	
Terrain:	9	
Date Walk Break:	10	

Sunday

Goal	1	Comments
Run/Walk/Run strategy used:	2	
Time:	3	
Distance:	4	
AM Pulse:	5	
Weather:	6	
Temp:	7	
Time: AM PM	8	
Terrain:	9	
Date Walk Break:	10	

Week of _____

WHEN I FINISH A RUN, EVERY PART OF ME IS SMILING.

Sc = standard course; in = injury; sp = speed; I = long run; sn = scenic; tr = transcendental; gr = group run; adj = adjustment; fn = fun; fb = fat burning; nu = nutrition
mn = mental training; ag = afterglow; so = social

Monday

Goal	1	Comments
Run/Walk/Run strategy used:		
	2	
Time:	3	
Distance:	4	
AM Pulse:	5	
Weather:	6	
Temp:	7	
Time: AM PM	8	
Terrain:	9	
Date Walk Break:	10	

Tuesday

Goal	1	Comments
Run/Walk/Run strategy used:		
	2	
Time:	3	
Distance:	4	
AM Pulse:	5	
Weather:	6	
Temp:	7	
Time: AM PM	8	
Terrain:	9	
Date Walk Break:	10	

Wednesday

Goal	1	Comments
Run/Walk/Run strategy used:		
	2	
Time:	3	
Distance:	4	
AM Pulse:	5	
Weather:	6	
Temp:	7	
Time: AM PM	8	
Terrain:	9	
Date Walk Break:	10	

Thursday

Goal	1	Comments
Run/Walk/Run strategy used:	2	
Time:	3	
Distance:	4	
AM Pulse:	5	
Weather:	6	
Temp:	7	
Time: AM PM	8	
Terrain:	9	
Date Walk Break:	10	

Friday

Goal	1	Comments
Run/Walk/Run strategy used:	2	
Time:	3	
Distance:	4	
AM Pulse:	5	
Weather:	6	
Temp:	7	
Time: AM PM	8	
Terrain:	9	
Date Walk Break:	10	

Saturday

Goal	1	Comments
Run/Walk/Run strategy used:	2	
Time:	3	
Distance:	4	
AM Pulse:	5	
Weather:	6	
Temp:	7	
Time: AM PM	8	
Terrain:	9	
Date Walk Break:	10	

Sunday

Goal	1	Comments
Run/Walk/Run strategy used:	2	
Time:	3	
Distance:	4	
AM Pulse:	5	
Weather:	6	
Temp:	7	
Time: AM PM	8	
Terrain:	9	
Date Walk Break:	10	

Week of _____

THE GLOW, AFTER A MORNING RUN, MAKES ME FEEL CLEAN ALL DAY.

Sc = standard course; in = injury; sp = speed; l = long run; sn = scenic; tr = transcendental; gr = group run; adj = adjustment; fn = fun; fb = fat burning; nu = nutrition
mn = mental training; ag = afterglow; so = social

Monday

Goal	1	Comments
Run/Walk/Run strategy used:	2	
Time:	3	
Distance:	4	
AM Pulse:	5	
Weather:	6	
Temp:	7	
Time: AM PM	8	
Terrain:	9	
Date Walk Break:	10	

Tuesday

Goal	1	Comments
Run/Walk/Run strategy used:	2	
Time:	3	
Distance:	4	
AM Pulse:	5	
Weather:	6	
Temp:	7	
Time: AM PM	8	
Terrain:	9	
Date Walk Break:	10	

Wednesday

Goal	1	Comments
Run/Walk/Run strategy used:	2	
Time:	3	
Distance:	4	
AM Pulse:	5	
Weather:	6	
Temp:	7	
Time: AM PM	8	
Terrain:	9	
Date Walk Break:	10	

Thursday

Goal	1	Comments
Run/Walk/Run strategy used:	2	
Time:	3	
Distance:	4	
AM Pulse:	5	
Weather:	6	
Temp:	7	
Time: AM PM	8	
Terrain:	9	
Date Walk Break:	10	

Friday

Goal	1	Comments
Run/Walk/Run strategy used:	2	
Time:	3	
Distance:	4	
AM Pulse:	5	
Weather:	6	
Temp:	7	
Time: AM PM	8	
Terrain:	9	
Date Walk Break:	10	

Saturday

Goal	1	Comments
Run/Walk/Run strategy used:	2	
Time:	3	
Distance:	4	
AM Pulse:	5	
Weather:	6	
Temp:	7	
Time: AM PM	8	
Terrain:	9	
Date Walk Break:	10	

Sunday

Goal	1	Comments
Run/Walk/Run strategy used:	2	
Time:	3	
Distance:	4	
AM Pulse:	5	
Weather:	6	
Temp:	7	
Time: AM PM	8	
Terrain:	9	
Date Walk Break:	10	

Week of _____

A SLOW RUN AT THE END OF THE DAY WILL DISCONNECT YOU FROM THE NEGATIVE AND ENERGIZE THE POSITIVE.

Sc = standard course; in = injury; sp = speed; l = long run; sn = scenic; tr = transcendental;
gr = group run; adj = adjustment; fn = fun; fb = fat burning; nu = nutrition
mn = mental training; ag = afterglow; so = social

Monday

Goal	1	Comments
Run/Walk/Run strategy used:	2	
Time:	3	
Distance:	4	
AM Pulse:	5	
Weather:	6	
Temp:	7	
Time: AM PM	8	
Terrain:	9	
Date — Walk Break:	10	

Tuesday

Goal	1	Comments
Run/Walk/Run strategy used:	2	
Time:	3	
Distance:	4	
AM Pulse:	5	
Weather:	6	
Temp:	7	
Time: AM PM	8	
Terrain:	9	
Date — Walk Break:	10	

Wednesday

Goal	1	Comments
Run/Walk/Run strategy used:	2	
Time:	3	
Distance:	4	
AM Pulse:	5	
Weather:	6	
Temp:	7	
Time: AM PM	8	
Terrain:	9	
Date — Walk Break:	10	

Thursday

Goal	1	Comments
Run/Walk/Run strategy used:	2	
Time:	3	
Distance:	4	
AM Pulse:	5	
Weather:	6	
Temp:	7	
Time: AM PM	8	
Terrain:	9	
Date Walk Break:	10	

Friday

Goal	1	Comments
Run/Walk/Run strategy used:	2	
Time:	3	
Distance:	4	
AM Pulse:	5	
Weather:	6	
Temp:	7	
Time: AM PM	8	
Terrain:	9	
Date Walk Break:	10	

Saturday

Goal	1	Comments
Run/Walk/Run strategy used:	2	
Time:	3	
Distance:	4	
AM Pulse:	5	
Weather:	6	
Temp:	7	
Time: AM PM	8	
Terrain:	9	
Date Walk Break:	10	

Sunday

Goal	1	Comments
Run/Walk/Run strategy used:	2	
Time:	3	
Distance:	4	
AM Pulse:	5	
Weather:	6	
Temp:	7	
Time: AM PM	8	
Terrain:	9	
Date Walk Break:	10	

Week of _____

RUNNING FOR 45 MINUTES OR MORE HELPS TO "FORMAT" YOUR BRAIN. AFTERWARDS YOU'RE BETTER PREPARED TO DEAL WITH STRESS, MANAGE CONFLICT, AND ACCEPT YOUR CHALLENGES WITH CREATIVITY AND ENERGY

Sc = standard course; in = injury; sp = speed; l = long run; sn = scenic; tr = transcendental;
gr = group run; adj = adjustment; fn = fun; fb = fat burning; nu = nutrition
mn = mental training; ag = afterglow; so = social

Monday

Goal	1	Comments
Run/Walk/Run strategy used:	2	
Time:	3	
Distance:	4	
AM Pulse:	5	
Weather:	6	
Temp:	7	
Time: AM PM	8	
Terrain:	9	
Date — Walk Break:	10	

Tuesday

Goal	1	Comments
Run/Walk/Run strategy used:	2	
Time:	3	
Distance:	4	
AM Pulse:	5	
Weather:	6	
Temp:	7	
Time: AM PM	8	
Terrain:	9	
Date — Walk Break:	10	

Wednesday

Goal	1	Comments
Run/Walk/Run strategy used:	2	
Time:	3	
Distance:	4	
AM Pulse:	5	
Weather:	6	
Temp:	7	
Time: AM PM	8	
Terrain:	9	
Date — Walk Break:	10	

Thursday

Goal	1	Comments
Run/Walk/Run strategy used:	2	
Time:	3	
Distance:	4	
AM Pulse:	5	
Weather:	6	
Temp:	7	
Time: ___ AM PM	8	
Terrain:	9	
Date Walk Break:	10	

Friday

Goal	1	Comments
Run/Walk/Run strategy used:	2	
Time:	3	
Distance:	4	
AM Pulse:	5	
Weather:	6	
Temp:	7	
Time: ___ AM PM	8	
Terrain:	9	
Date Walk Break:	10	

Saturday

Goal	1	Comments
Run/Walk/Run strategy used:	2	
Time:	3	
Distance:	4	
AM Pulse:	5	
Weather:	6	
Temp:	7	
Time: ___ AM PM	8	
Terrain:	9	
Date Walk Break:	10	

Sunday

Goal	1	Comments
Run/Walk/Run strategy used:	2	
Time:	3	
Distance:	4	
AM Pulse:	5	
Weather:	6	
Temp:	7	
Time: ___ AM PM	8	
Terrain:	9	
Date Walk Break:	10	

Week of _____

A SLOW START CAN MAKE ALMOST EVERY RUN A GOOD ONE.
I START EVERY RUN AT LEAST THREE MINUTES PER MILE SLOWER
THAN I COULD RACE THE DISTANCE I'M PLANNING TO RUN THAT DAY.

Sc = standard course; in = injury; sp = speed; l = long run; sn = scenic; tr = transcendental; gr = group run; adj = adjustment; fn = fun; fb = fat burning; nu = nutrition mn = mental training; ag = afterglow; so = social

Monday			Comments
Goal		1	
Run/Walk/Run strategy used:		2	
Time:		3	
Distance:		4	
AM Pulse:		5	
Weather:		6	
Temp:		7	
Time:	AM PM	8	
Terrain:		9	
Date	Walk Break:	10	

Tuesday			Comments
Goal		1	
Run/Walk/Run strategy used:		2	
Time:		3	
Distance:		4	
AM Pulse:		5	
Weather:		6	
Temp:		7	
Time:	AM PM	8	
Terrain:		9	
Date	Walk Break:	10	

Wednesday			Comments
Goal		1	
Run/Walk/Run strategy used:		2	
Time:		3	
Distance:		4	
AM Pulse:		5	
Weather:		6	
Temp:		7	
Time:	AM PM	8	
Terrain:		9	
Date	Walk Break:	10	

Thursday

			Comments
Goal		1	
Run/Walk/Run strategy used:		2	
Time:		3	
Distance:		4	
AM Pulse:		5	
Weather:		6	
Temp:		7	
Time:	AM PM	8	
Terrain:		9	
Date	Walk Break:	10	

Friday

			Comments
Goal		1	
Run/Walk/Run strategy used:		2	
Time:		3	
Distance:		4	
AM Pulse:		5	
Weather:		6	
Temp:		7	
Time:	AM PM	8	
Terrain:		9	
Date	Walk Break:	10	

Saturday

			Comments
Goal		1	
Run/Walk/Run strategy used:		2	
Time:		3	
Distance:		4	
AM Pulse:		5	
Weather:		6	
Temp:		7	
Time:	AM PM	8	
Terrain:		9	
Date	Walk Break:	10	

Sunday

			Comments
Goal		1	
Run/Walk/Run strategy used:		2	
Time:		3	
Distance:		4	
AM Pulse:		5	
Weather:		6	
Temp:		7	
Time:	AM PM	8	
Terrain:		9	
Date	Walk Break:	10	

Week of _____

YOU ARE CAPABLE OF BECOMING A RUNNING SUCCESS EVERY DAY. ALL YOU NEED TO DO IS TO MOVE FORWARD BY WALKING AND/OR RUNNING FAR ENOUGH FOR THE ENDORPHINS AND THE SATISFACTION TO POUR OUT

Sc = standard course; in = injury; sp = speed; l = long run; sn = scenic; tr = transcendental; gr = group run; adj = adjustment; fn = fun; fb = fat burning; nu = nutrition
mn = mental training; ag = afterglow; so = social

Monday

Goal	1	Comments
Run/Walk/Run strategy used:	2	
Time:	3	
Distance:	4	
AM Pulse:	5	
Weather:	6	
Temp:	7	
Time: AM PM	8	
Terrain:	9	
Date Walk Break:	10	

Tuesday

Goal	1	Comments
Run/Walk/Run strategy used:	2	
Time:	3	
Distance:	4	
AM Pulse:	5	
Weather:	6	
Temp:	7	
Time: AM PM	8	
Terrain:	9	
Date Walk Break:	10	

Wednesday

Goal	1	Comments
Run/Walk/Run strategy used:	2	
Time:	3	
Distance:	4	
AM Pulse:	5	
Weather:	6	
Temp:	7	
Time: AM PM	8	
Terrain:	9	
Date Walk Break:	10	

Thursday

Goal	1	Comments
Run/Walk/Run strategy used:	2	
Time:	3	
Distance:	4	
AM Pulse:	5	
Weather:	6	
Temp:	7	
Time: AM PM	8	
Terrain:	9	
Date Walk Break:	10	

Friday

Goal	1	Comments
Run/Walk/Run strategy used:	2	
Time:	3	
Distance:	4	
AM Pulse:	5	
Weather:	6	
Temp:	7	
Time: AM PM	8	
Terrain:	9	
Date Walk Break:	10	

Saturday

Goal	1	Comments
Run/Walk/Run strategy used:	2	
Time:	3	
Distance:	4	
AM Pulse:	5	
Weather:	6	
Temp:	7	
Time: AM PM	8	
Terrain:	9	
Date Walk Break:	10	

Sunday

Goal	1	Comments
Run/Walk/Run strategy used:	2	
Time:	3	
Distance:	4	
AM Pulse:	5	
Weather:	6	
Temp:	7	
Time: AM PM	8	
Terrain:	9	
Date Walk Break:	10	

Week of _____

AS YOU FIND NEW WAYS TO ENJOY DAILY RUNS, YOU BECOME MORE COMMITTED TO FITNESS.

Sc = standard course; in = injury; sp = speed; l = long run; sn = scenic; tr = transcendental; gr = group run; adj = adjustment; fn = fun; fb = fat burning; nu = nutrition
mn = mental training; ag = afterglow; so = social

Monday

			Comments
Goal		1	
Run/Walk/Run strategy used:		2	
Time:		3	
Distance:		4	
AM Pulse:		5	
Weather:		6	
Temp:		7	
Time:	AM PM	8	
Terrain:		9	
Date	Walk Break:	10	

Tuesday

			Comments
Goal		1	
Run/Walk/Run strategy used:		2	
Time:		3	
Distance:		4	
AM Pulse:		5	
Weather:		6	
Temp:		7	
Time:	AM PM	8	
Terrain:		9	
Date	Walk Break:	10	

Wednesday

			Comments
Goal		1	
Run/Walk/Run strategy used:		2	
Time:		3	
Distance:		4	
AM Pulse:		5	
Weather:		6	
Temp:		7	
Time:	AM PM	8	
Terrain:		9	
Date	Walk Break:	10	

Thursday

			Comments
Goal		1	
Run/Walk/Run strategy used:		2	
Time:		3	
Distance:		4	
AM Pulse:		5	
Weather:		6	
Temp:		7	
Time:	AM PM	8	
Terrain:		9	
Date	Walk Break:	10	

Friday

			Comments
Goal		1	
Run/Walk/Run strategy used:		2	
Time:		3	
Distance:		4	
AM Pulse:		5	
Weather:		6	
Temp:		7	
Time:	AM PM	8	
Terrain:		9	
Date	Walk Break:	10	

Saturday

			Comments
Goal		1	
Run/Walk/Run strategy used:		2	
Time:		3	
Distance:		4	
AM Pulse:		5	
Weather:		6	
Temp:		7	
Time:	AM PM	8	
Terrain:		9	
Date	Walk Break:	10	

Sunday

			Comments
Goal		1	
Run/Walk/Run strategy used:		2	
Time:		3	
Distance:		4	
AM Pulse:		5	
Weather:		6	
Temp:		7	
Time:	AM PM	8	
Terrain:		9	
Date	Walk Break:	10	

Week of _____

THE TIME TO YOURSELF DURING A WALK OR RUN CAN RESTORE AND STRENGTHEN YOU BY HELPING YOU TO COMMUNICATE WITH YOURSELF.

Sc = standard course; in = injury; sp = speed; l = long run; sn = scenic; tr = transcendental; gr = group run; adj = adjustment; fn = fun; fb = fat burning; nu = nutrition
mn = mental training; ag = afterglow; so = social

Monday

Goal		1	Comments
Run/Walk/Run strategy used:		2	
Time:		3	
Distance:		4	
AM Pulse:		5	
Weather:		6	
Temp:		7	
Time:	AM PM	8	
Terrain:		9	
Date Walk Break:		10	

Tuesday

Goal		1	Comments
Run/Walk/Run strategy used:		2	
Time:		3	
Distance:		4	
AM Pulse:		5	
Weather:		6	
Temp:		7	
Time:	AM PM	8	
Terrain:		9	
Date Walk Break:		10	

Wednesday

Goal		1	Comments
Run/Walk/Run strategy used:		2	
Time:		3	
Distance:		4	
AM Pulse:		5	
Weather:		6	
Temp:		7	
Time:	AM PM	8	
Terrain:		9	
Date Walk Break:		10	

Thursday

Goal	1	Comments
Run/Walk/Run strategy used:	2	
Time:	3	
Distance:	4	
AM Pulse:	5	
Weather:	6	
Temp:	7	
Time: AM PM	8	
Terrain:	9	
Date Walk Break:	10	

Friday

Goal	1	Comments
Run/Walk/Run strategy used:	2	
Time:	3	
Distance:	4	
AM Pulse:	5	
Weather:	6	
Temp:	7	
Time: AM PM	8	
Terrain:	9	
Date Walk Break:	10	

Saturday

Goal	1	Comments
Run/Walk/Run strategy used:	2	
Time:	3	
Distance:	4	
AM Pulse:	5	
Weather:	6	
Temp:	7	
Time: AM PM	8	
Terrain:	9	
Date Walk Break:	10	

Sunday

Goal	1	Comments
Run/Walk/Run strategy used:	2	
Time:	3	
Distance:	4	
AM Pulse:	5	
Weather:	6	
Temp:	7	
Time: AM PM	8	
Terrain:	9	
Date Walk Break:	10	

Week of _____

FORWARD MOTION EXERTION UNLEASHES A SERIES OF REWARDS WHICH KEEP ON GIVING AS LONG AS YOU CONTINUE TO EXERCISE REGULARLY.

Sc = standard course; in = injury; sp = speed; l = long run; sn = scenic; tr = transcendental; gr = group run; adj = adjustment; fn = fun; fb = fat burning; nu = nutrition
mn = mental training; ag = afterglow; so = social

Monday

Goal		1	Comments
Run/Walk/Run strategy used:		2	
Time:		3	
Distance:		4	
AM Pulse:		5	
Weather:		6	
Temp:		7	
Time:	AM PM	8	
Terrain:		9	
Date	Walk Break:	10	

Tuesday

Goal		1	Comments
Run/Walk/Run strategy used:		2	
Time:		3	
Distance:		4	
AM Pulse:		5	
Weather:		6	
Temp:		7	
Time:	AM PM	8	
Terrain:		9	
Date	Walk Break:	10	

Wednesday

Goal		1	Comments
Run/Walk/Run strategy used:		2	
Time:		3	
Distance:		4	
AM Pulse:		5	
Weather:		6	
Temp:		7	
Time:	AM PM	8	
Terrain:		9	
Date	Walk Break:	10	

Thursday

Goal	1	Comments
Run/Walk/Run strategy used:	2	
Time:	3	
Distance:	4	
AM Pulse:	5	
Weather:	6	
Temp:	7	
Time: AM PM	8	
Terrain:	9	
Date Walk Break:	10	

Friday

Goal	1	Comments
Run/Walk/Run strategy used:	2	
Time:	3	
Distance:	4	
AM Pulse:	5	
Weather:	6	
Temp:	7	
Time: AM PM	8	
Terrain:	9	
Date Walk Break:	10	

Saturday

Goal	1	Comments
Run/Walk/Run strategy used:	2	
Time:	3	
Distance:	4	
AM Pulse:	5	
Weather:	6	
Temp:	7	
Time: AM PM	8	
Terrain:	9	
Date Walk Break:	10	

Sunday

Goal	1	Comments
Run/Walk/Run strategy used:	2	
Time:	3	
Distance:	4	
AM Pulse:	5	
Weather:	6	
Temp:	7	
Time: AM PM	8	
Terrain:	9	
Date Walk Break:	10	

Week of _____

THE MOST EXHILARATING RUNS ARE OFTEN
ON THE STRESSED OUT DAYS WHEN WE DON'T WANT TO RUN.

Sc = standard course; in = injury; sp = speed; l = long run; sn = scenic; tr = transcendental; gr = group run; adj = adjustment; fn = fun; fb = fat burning; nu = nutrition
mn = mental training; ag = afterglow; so = social

Monday

Goal		1	Comments
Run/Walk/Run strategy used:		2	
Time:		3	
Distance:		4	
AM Pulse:		5	
Weather:		6	
Temp:		7	
Time:	AM PM	8	
Terrain:		9	
Date	Walk Break:	10	

Tuesday

Goal		1	Comments
Run/Walk/Run strategy used:		2	
Time:		3	
Distance:		4	
AM Pulse:		5	
Weather:		6	
Temp:		7	
Time:	AM PM	8	
Terrain:		9	
Date	Walk Break:	10	

Wednesday

Goal		1	Comments
Run/Walk/Run strategy used:		2	
Time:		3	
Distance:		4	
AM Pulse:		5	
Weather:		6	
Temp:		7	
Time:	AM PM	8	
Terrain:		9	
Date	Walk Break:	10	

Thursday	Goal	1	Comments
	Run/Walk/Run strategy used:	2	
	Time:	3	
	Distance:	4	
	AM Pulse:	5	
	Weather:	6	
	Temp:	7	
	Time: AM PM	8	
	Terrain:	9	
Date	Walk Break:	10	

Friday	Goal	1	Comments
	Run/Walk/Run strategy used:	2	
	Time:	3	
	Distance:	4	
	AM Pulse:	5	
	Weather:	6	
	Temp:	7	
	Time: AM PM	8	
	Terrain:	9	
Date	Walk Break:	10	

Saturday	Goal	1	Comments
	Run/Walk/Run strategy used:	2	
	Time:	3	
	Distance:	4	
	AM Pulse:	5	
	Weather:	6	
	Temp:	7	
	Time: AM PM	8	
	Terrain:	9	
Date	Walk Break:	10	

Sunday	Goal	1	Comments
	Run/Walk/Run strategy used:	2	
	Time:	3	
	Distance:	4	
	AM Pulse:	5	
	Weather:	6	
	Temp:	7	
	Time: AM PM	8	
	Terrain:	9	
Date	Walk Break:	10	

Week of _____

AS WE MATURE, WE BECOME INTROSPECTIVE. RUNNING ALLOWS THIS INNER COMMUNICATION TO TAKE PLACE IN A POSITIVE ENVIRONMENT, PRODUCING POSITIVE MOMENTUM IN ALL AREAS OF LIFE.

Sc = standard course; in = injury; sp = speed; l = long run; sn = scenic; tr = transcendental; gr = group run; adj = adjustment; fn = fun; fb = fat burning; nu = nutrition mn = mental training; ag = afterglow; so = social

Monday

Goal	1	Comments
Run/Walk/Run strategy used:	2	
Time:	3	
Distance:	4	
AM Pulse:	5	
Weather:	6	
Temp:	7	
Time: ___ AM PM	8	
Terrain:	9	
Date Walk Break:	10	

Tuesday

Goal	1	Comments
Run/Walk/Run strategy used:	2	
Time:	3	
Distance:	4	
AM Pulse:	5	
Weather:	6	
Temp:	7	
Time: ___ AM PM	8	
Terrain:	9	
Date Walk Break:	10	

Wednesday

Goal	1	Comments
Run/Walk/Run strategy used:	2	
Time:	3	
Distance:	4	
AM Pulse:	5	
Weather:	6	
Temp:	7	
Time: ___ AM PM	8	
Terrain:	9	
Date Walk Break:	10	

Thursday

Goal	1	Comments
Run/Walk/Run strategy used:	2	
Time:	3	
Distance:	4	
AM Pulse:	5	
Weather:	6	
Temp:	7	
Time: AM PM	8	
Terrain:	9	
Date Walk Break:	10	

Friday

Goal	1	Comments
Run/Walk/Run strategy used:	2	
Time:	3	
Distance:	4	
AM Pulse:	5	
Weather:	6	
Temp:	7	
Time: AM PM	8	
Terrain:	9	
Date Walk Break:	10	

Saturday

Goal	1	Comments
Run/Walk/Run strategy used:	2	
Time:	3	
Distance:	4	
AM Pulse:	5	
Weather:	6	
Temp:	7	
Time: AM PM	8	
Terrain:	9	
Date Walk Break:	10	

Sunday

Goal	1	Comments
Run/Walk/Run strategy used:	2	
Time:	3	
Distance:	4	
AM Pulse:	5	
Weather:	6	
Temp:	7	
Time: AM PM	8	
Terrain:	9	
Date Walk Break:	10	

Week of _____

EVEN AFTER THE MOST STRESSFUL DAY, A SLOW 60-MINUTE RUN LEAVES ME FEELING POSITIVE ABOUT MYSELF AND THE FUTURE.

Sc = standard course; in = injury; sp = speed; l = long run; sn = scenic; tr = transcendental; gr = group run; adj = adjustment; fn = fun; fb = fat burning; nu = nutrition
mn = mental training; ag = afterglow; so = social

Monday

Goal		1	Comments
Run/Walk/Run strategy used:		2	
Time:		3	
Distance:		4	
AM Pulse:		5	
Weather:		6	
Temp:		7	
Time:	AM PM	8	
Terrain:		9	
Date — Walk Break:		10	

Tuesday

Goal		1	Comments
Run/Walk/Run strategy used:		2	
Time:		3	
Distance:		4	
AM Pulse:		5	
Weather:		6	
Temp:		7	
Time:	AM PM	8	
Terrain:		9	
Date — Walk Break:		10	

Wednesday

Goal		1	Comments
Run/Walk/Run strategy used:		2	
Time:		3	
Distance:		4	
AM Pulse:		5	
Weather:		6	
Temp:		7	
Time:	AM PM	8	
Terrain:		9	
Date — Walk Break:		10	

Thursday

Goal	1	Comments
Run/Walk/Run strategy used:	2	
Time:	3	
Distance:	4	
AM Pulse:	5	
Weather:	6	
Temp:	7	
Time: AM PM	8	
Terrain:	9	
Date Walk Break:	10	

Friday

Goal	1	Comments
Run/Walk/Run strategy used:	2	
Time:	3	
Distance:	4	
AM Pulse:	5	
Weather:	6	
Temp:	7	
Time: AM PM	8	
Terrain:	9	
Date Walk Break:	10	

Saturday

Goal	1	Comments
Run/Walk/Run strategy used:	2	
Time:	3	
Distance:	4	
AM Pulse:	5	
Weather:	6	
Temp:	7	
Time: AM PM	8	
Terrain:	9	
Date Walk Break:	10	

Sunday

Goal	1	Comments
Run/Walk/Run strategy used:	2	
Time:	3	
Distance:	4	
AM Pulse:	5	
Weather:	6	
Temp:	7	
Time: AM PM	8	
Terrain:	9	
Date Walk Break:	10	

Week of _____

WE ARE DESIGNED TO RUN – AND WE INCREASE OUR CHANCE OF DAILY HAPPINESS WHEN WE DO SO.

Sc = standard course; in = injury; sp = speed; l = long run; sn = scenic; tr = transcendental; gr = group run; adj = adjustment; fn = fun; fb = fat burning; nu = nutrition mn = mental training; ag = afterglow; so = social

Monday

Goal	1	Comments
Run/Walk/Run strategy used:	2	
Time:	3	
Distance:	4	
AM Pulse:	5	
Weather:	6	
Temp:	7	
Time: AM PM	8	
Terrain:	9	
Date Walk Break:	10	

Tuesday

Goal	1	Comments
Run/Walk/Run strategy used:	2	
Time:	3	
Distance:	4	
AM Pulse:	5	
Weather:	6	
Temp:	7	
Time: AM PM	8	
Terrain:	9	
Date Walk Break:	10	

Wednesday

Goal	1	Comments
Run/Walk/Run strategy used:	2	
Time:	3	
Distance:	4	
AM Pulse:	5	
Weather:	6	
Temp:	7	
Time: AM PM	8	
Terrain:	9	
Date Walk Break:	10	

Thursday

Goal	1	Comments
Run/Walk/Run strategy used:	2	
Time:	3	
Distance:	4	
AM Pulse:	5	
Weather:	6	
Temp:	7	
Time: AM PM	8	
Terrain:	9	
Date Walk Break:	10	

Friday

Goal	1	Comments
Run/Walk/Run strategy used:	2	
Time:	3	
Distance:	4	
AM Pulse:	5	
Weather:	6	
Temp:	7	
Time: AM PM	8	
Terrain:	9	
Date Walk Break:	10	

Saturday

Goal	1	Comments
Run/Walk/Run strategy used:	2	
Time:	3	
Distance:	4	
AM Pulse:	5	
Weather:	6	
Temp:	7	
Time: AM PM	8	
Terrain:	9	
Date Walk Break:	10	

Sunday

Goal	1	Comments
Run/Walk/Run strategy used:	2	
Time:	3	
Distance:	4	
AM Pulse:	5	
Weather:	6	
Temp:	7	
Time: AM PM	8	
Terrain:	9	
Date Walk Break:	10	

Week of _____

RUNNING IS ONE OF THE BEST WAYS TO GET YOUR RIGHT BRAIN IN GEAR, TO INSPIRE CREATIVITY.

Sc = standard course; in = injury; sp = speed; l = long run; sn = scenic; tr = transcendental;
gr = group run; adj = adjustment; fn = fun; fb = fat burning; nu = nutrition
mn = mental training; ag = afterglow; so = social

Monday			
	Goal	1	Comments
	Run/Walk/Run strategy used:	2	
	Time:	3	
	Distance:	4	
	AM Pulse:	5	
	Weather:	6	
	Temp:	7	
	Time: AM PM	8	
	Terrain:	9	
Date	Walk Break:	10	

Tuesday			
	Goal	1	Comments
	Run/Walk/Run strategy used:	2	
	Time:	3	
	Distance:	4	
	AM Pulse:	5	
	Weather:	6	
	Temp:	7	
	Time: AM PM	8	
	Terrain:	9	
Date	Walk Break:	10	

Wednesday			
	Goal	1	Comments
	Run/Walk/Run strategy used:	2	
	Time:	3	
	Distance:	4	
	AM Pulse:	5	
	Weather:	6	
	Temp:	7	
	Time: AM PM	8	
	Terrain:	9	
Date	Walk Break:	10	

Thursday

Goal	1	Comments
Run/Walk/Run strategy used:	2	
Time:	3	
Distance:	4	
AM Pulse:	5	
Weather:	6	
Temp:	7	
Time: AM PM	8	
Terrain:	9	
Date Walk Break:	10	

Friday

Goal	1	Comments
Run/Walk/Run strategy used:	2	
Time:	3	
Distance:	4	
AM Pulse:	5	
Weather:	6	
Temp:	7	
Time: AM PM	8	
Terrain:	9	
Date Walk Break:	10	

Saturday

Goal	1	Comments
Run/Walk/Run strategy used:	2	
Time:	3	
Distance:	4	
AM Pulse:	5	
Weather:	6	
Temp:	7	
Time: AM PM	8	
Terrain:	9	
Date Walk Break:	10	

Sunday

Goal	1	Comments
Run/Walk/Run strategy used:	2	
Time:	3	
Distance:	4	
AM Pulse:	5	
Weather:	6	
Temp:	7	
Time: AM PM	8	
Terrain:	9	
Date Walk Break:	10	

Week of _____

RUNNING INSPIRES A SERIES OF POSITIVE AND MOTIVATIONAL CHANGES INSIDE OF US – RUNNERS ARE MORE POSITIVE PEOPLE.

Sc = standard course; in = injury; sp = speed; l = long run; sn = scenic; tr = transcendental; gr = group run; adj = adjustment; fn = fun; fb = fat burning; nu = nutrition
mn = mental training; ag = afterglow; so = social

Monday

Goal		1	Comments
Run/Walk/Run strategy used:		2	
Time:		3	
Distance:		4	
AM Pulse:		5	
Weather:		6	
Temp:		7	
Time:	AM PM	8	
Terrain:		9	
Walk Break:		10	

Date

Tuesday

Goal		1	Comments
Run/Walk/Run strategy used:		2	
Time:		3	
Distance:		4	
AM Pulse:		5	
Weather:		6	
Temp:		7	
Time:	AM PM	8	
Terrain:		9	
Walk Break:		10	

Date

Wednesday

Goal		1	Comments
Run/Walk/Run strategy used:		2	
Time:		3	
Distance:		4	
AM Pulse:		5	
Weather:		6	
Temp:		7	
Time:	AM PM	8	
Terrain:		9	
Walk Break:		10	

Date

Thursday

Goal	1	Comments
Run/Walk/Run strategy used:	2	
Time:	3	
Distance:	4	
AM Pulse:	5	
Weather:	6	
Temp:	7	
Time: AM PM	8	
Terrain:	9	
Walk Break:	10	

Date

Friday

Goal	1	Comments
Run/Walk/Run strategy used:	2	
Time:	3	
Distance:	4	
AM Pulse:	5	
Weather:	6	
Temp:	7	
Time: AM PM	8	
Terrain:	9	
Walk Break:	10	

Date

Saturday

Goal	1	Comments
Run/Walk/Run strategy used:	2	
Time:	3	
Distance:	4	
AM Pulse:	5	
Weather:	6	
Temp:	7	
Time: AM PM	8	
Terrain:	9	
Walk Break:	10	

Date

Sunday

Goal	1	Comments
Run/Walk/Run strategy used:	2	
Time:	3	
Distance:	4	
AM Pulse:	5	
Weather:	6	
Temp:	7	
Time: AM PM	8	
Terrain:	9	
Walk Break:	10	

Date

Week of _____

OUR ANCIENT ANCESTORS DESIGNED US TO BE RUNNERS AND WALKERS. WHEN WE DO SO WE GO BACK TO OUR ROOTS AND FEEL A GREAT SENSE OF FULFILLMENT.

Sc = standard course; in = injury; sp = speed; l = long run; sn = scenic; tr = transcendental; gr = group run; adj = adjustment; fn = fun; fb = fat burning; nu = nutrition
mn = mental training; ag = afterglow; so = social

Monday

Goal	1	Comments
Run/Walk/Run strategy used:	2	
Time:	3	
Distance:	4	
AM Pulse:	5	
Weather:	6	
Temp:	7	
Time: AM PM	8	
Terrain:	9	
Date	Walk Break:	10	

Tuesday

Goal	1	Comments
Run/Walk/Run strategy used:	2	
Time:	3	
Distance:	4	
AM Pulse:	5	
Weather:	6	
Temp:	7	
Time: AM PM	8	
Terrain:	9	
Date	Walk Break:	10	

Wednesday

Goal	1	Comments
Run/Walk/Run strategy used:	2	
Time:	3	
Distance:	4	
AM Pulse:	5	
Weather:	6	
Temp:	7	
Time: AM PM	8	
Terrain:	9	
Date	Walk Break:	10	

Thursday	Goal	1	Comments
	Run/Walk/Run strategy used:	2	
	Time:	3	
	Distance:	4	
	AM Pulse:	5	
	Weather:	6	
	Temp:	7	
	Time: AM PM	8	
	Terrain:	9	
Date	Walk Break:	10	

Friday	Goal	1	Comments
	Run/Walk/Run strategy used:	2	
	Time:	3	
	Distance:	4	
	AM Pulse:	5	
	Weather:	6	
	Temp:	7	
	Time: AM PM	8	
	Terrain:	9	
Date	Walk Break:	10	

Saturday	Goal	1	Comments
	Run/Walk/Run strategy used:	2	
	Time:	3	
	Distance:	4	
	AM Pulse:	5	
	Weather:	6	
	Temp:	7	
	Time: AM PM	8	
	Terrain:	9	
Date	Walk Break:	10	

Sunday	Goal	1	Comments
	Run/Walk/Run strategy used:	2	
	Time:	3	
	Distance:	4	
	AM Pulse:	5	
	Weather:	6	
	Temp:	7	
	Time: AM PM	8	
	Terrain:	9	
Date	Walk Break:	10	

Week of _____

TO MOVE FORWARD REGULARLY MAKES YOU FEEL GROUNDED, REAL AND NATURALLY ALIVE.

Sc = standard course; in = injury; sp = speed; I = long run; sn = scenic; tr = transcendental; gr = group run; adj = adjustment; fn = fun; fb = fat burning; nu = nutrition
mn = mental training; ag = afterglow; so = social

Monday

			Comments
Goal		1	
Run/Walk/Run strategy used:		2	
Time:		3	
Distance:		4	
AM Pulse:		5	
Weather:		6	
Temp:		7	
Time:	AM PM	8	
Terrain:		9	
Date	Walk Break:	10	

Tuesday

			Comments
Goal		1	
Run/Walk/Run strategy used:		2	
Time:		3	
Distance:		4	
AM Pulse:		5	
Weather:		6	
Temp:		7	
Time:	AM PM	8	
Terrain:		9	
Date	Walk Break:	10	

Wednesday

			Comments
Goal		1	
Run/Walk/Run strategy used:		2	
Time:		3	
Distance:		4	
AM Pulse:		5	
Weather:		6	
Temp:		7	
Time:	AM PM	8	
Terrain:		9	
Date	Walk Break:	10	

Thursday

Goal	1	Comments
Run/Walk/Run strategy used:	2	
Time:	3	
Distance:	4	
AM Pulse:	5	
Weather:	6	
Temp:	7	
Time: AM PM	8	
Terrain:	9	
Date Walk Break:	10	

Friday

Goal	1	Comments
Run/Walk/Run strategy used:	2	
Time:	3	
Distance:	4	
AM Pulse:	5	
Weather:	6	
Temp:	7	
Time: AM PM	8	
Terrain:	9	
Date Walk Break:	10	

Saturday

Goal	1	Comments
Run/Walk/Run strategy used:	2	
Time:	3	
Distance:	4	
AM Pulse:	5	
Weather:	6	
Temp:	7	
Time: AM PM	8	
Terrain:	9	
Date Walk Break:	10	

Sunday

Goal	1	Comments
Run/Walk/Run strategy used:	2	
Time:	3	
Distance:	4	
AM Pulse:	5	
Weather:	6	
Temp:	7	
Time: AM PM	8	
Terrain:	9	
Date Walk Break:	10	

Week of _____

IT'S POSSIBLE TO COMPLETELY TURN AROUND
A NONPRODUCTIVE ATTITUDE DURING A RUN.

Sc = standard course; in = injury; sp = speed; I = long run; sn = scenic; tr = transcendental; gr = group run; adj = adjustment; fn = fun; fb = fat burning; nu = nutrition mn = mental training; ag = afterglow; so = social

Monday

Goal	1	Comments
Run/Walk/Run strategy used:	2	
Time:	3	
Distance:	4	
AM Pulse:	5	
Weather:	6	
Temp:	7	
Time: AM PM	8	
Terrain:	9	
Date Walk Break:	10	

Tuesday

Goal	1	Comments
Run/Walk/Run strategy used:	2	
Time:	3	
Distance:	4	
AM Pulse:	5	
Weather:	6	
Temp:	7	
Time: AM PM	8	
Terrain:	9	
Date Walk Break:	10	

Wednesday

Goal	1	Comments
Run/Walk/Run strategy used:	2	
Time:	3	
Distance:	4	
AM Pulse:	5	
Weather:	6	
Temp:	7	
Time: AM PM	8	
Terrain:	9	
Date Walk Break:	10	

Thursday

Goal	1	Comments
Run/Walk/Run strategy used:	2	
Time:	3	
Distance:	4	
AM Pulse:	5	
Weather:	6	
Temp:	7	
Time: AM PM	8	
Terrain:	9	
Date Walk Break:	10	

Friday

Goal	1	Comments
Run/Walk/Run strategy used:	2	
Time:	3	
Distance:	4	
AM Pulse:	5	
Weather:	6	
Temp:	7	
Time: AM PM	8	
Terrain:	9	
Date Walk Break:	10	

Saturday

Goal	1	Comments
Run/Walk/Run strategy used:	2	
Time:	3	
Distance:	4	
AM Pulse:	5	
Weather:	6	
Temp:	7	
Time: AM PM	8	
Terrain:	9	
Date Walk Break:	10	

Sunday

Goal	1	Comments
Run/Walk/Run strategy used:	2	
Time:	3	
Distance:	4	
AM Pulse:	5	
Weather:	6	
Temp:	7	
Time: AM PM	8	
Terrain:	9	
Date Walk Break:	10	

Week of _____

YOU'LL TEACH YOURSELF TO RUN FASTER BY TAKING A VERY LIGHT AND QUICK TOUCH WITH EACH FOOT. THIS HELPS YOU INCREASE THE TURNOVE OF FEET AND LEGS, OFTEN WITH A SLIGHTLY SHORTER STRIDE LENGTH.

Sc = standard course; in = injury; sp = speed; l = long run; sn = scenic; tr = transcendental; gr = group run; adj = adjustment; fn = fun; fb = fat burning; nu = nutrition
mn = mental training; ag = afterglow; so = social

Monday

Goal	1	Comments
Run/Walk/Run strategy used:	2	
Time:	3	
Distance:	4	
AM Pulse:	5	
Weather:	6	
Temp:	7	
Time: AM PM	8	
Terrain:	9	
Date Walk Break:	10	

Tuesday

Goal	1	Comments
Run/Walk/Run strategy used:	2	
Time:	3	
Distance:	4	
AM Pulse:	5	
Weather:	6	
Temp:	7	
Time: AM PM	8	
Terrain:	9	
Date Walk Break:	10	

Wednesday

Goal	1	Comments
Run/Walk/Run strategy used:	2	
Time:	3	
Distance:	4	
AM Pulse:	5	
Weather:	6	
Temp:	7	
Time: AM PM	8	
Terrain:	9	
Date Walk Break:	10	

Thursday

Goal	1	Comments
Run/Walk/Run strategy used:	2	
Time:	3	
Distance:	4	
AM Pulse:	5	
Weather:	6	
Temp:	7	
Time: AM PM	8	
Terrain:	9	
Date Walk Break:	10	

Friday

Goal	1	Comments
Run/Walk/Run strategy used:	2	
Time:	3	
Distance:	4	
AM Pulse:	5	
Weather:	6	
Temp:	7	
Time: AM PM	8	
Terrain:	9	
Date Walk Break:	10	

Saturday

Goal	1	Comments
Run/Walk/Run strategy used:	2	
Time:	3	
Distance:	4	
AM Pulse:	5	
Weather:	6	
Temp:	7	
Time: AM PM	8	
Terrain:	9	
Date Walk Break:	10	

Sunday

Goal	1	Comments
Run/Walk/Run strategy used:	2	
Time:	3	
Distance:	4	
AM Pulse:	5	
Weather:	6	
Temp:	7	
Time: AM PM	8	
Terrain:	9	
Date Walk Break:	10	

Week of _____

WHEN YOU MAKE RUNNING MISTAKES, WRITE THEM DOWN AND MAKE CHANGES IN YOUR RUNNING WHICH WILL KEEP THEM FROM OCCURRING AGAIN.

Sc = standard course; in = injury; sp = speed; l = long run; sn = scenic; tr = transcendental; gr = group run; adj = adjustment; fn = fun; fb = fat burning; nu = nutrition mn = mental training; ag = afterglow; so = social

Monday

Goal	1	Comments
Run/Walk/Run strategy used:	2	
Time:	3	
Distance:	4	
AM Pulse:	5	
Weather:	6	
Temp:	7	
Time: AM PM	8	
Terrain:	9	
Date Walk Break:	10	

Tuesday

Goal	1	Comments
Run/Walk/Run strategy used:	2	
Time:	3	
Distance:	4	
AM Pulse:	5	
Weather:	6	
Temp:	7	
Time: AM PM	8	
Terrain:	9	
Date Walk Break:	10	

Wednesday

Goal	1	Comments
Run/Walk/Run strategy used:	2	
Time:	3	
Distance:	4	
AM Pulse:	5	
Weather:	6	
Temp:	7	
Time: AM PM	8	
Terrain:	9	
Date Walk Break:	10	

Thursday

Goal	1	Comments
Run/Walk/Run strategy used:	2	
Time:	3	
Distance:	4	
AM Pulse:	5	
Weather:	6	
Temp:	7	
Time: AM PM	8	
Terrain:	9	
Date Walk Break:	10	

Friday

Goal	1	Comments
Run/Walk/Run strategy used:	2	
Time:	3	
Distance:	4	
AM Pulse:	5	
Weather:	6	
Temp:	7	
Time: AM PM	8	
Terrain:	9	
Date Walk Break:	10	

Saturday

Goal	1	Comments
Run/Walk/Run strategy used:	2	
Time:	3	
Distance:	4	
AM Pulse:	5	
Weather:	6	
Temp:	7	
Time: AM PM	8	
Terrain:	9	
Date Walk Break:	10	

Sunday

Goal	1	Comments
Run/Walk/Run strategy used:	2	
Time:	3	
Distance:	4	
AM Pulse:	5	
Weather:	6	
Temp:	7	
Time: AM PM	8	
Terrain:	9	
Date Walk Break:	10	

Week of _____

RUNNING UP HILLS, AT RACE PACE, WILL STRENGTHEN YOUR LEGS BETTER THAN ANY WEIGHT TRAINING YOU COULD DO. WALK DOWN EACH HILL FOR COMPLETE RECOVERY, AND DO THIS SESSION ONLY ONCE A WEEK.

Sc = standard course; in = injury; sp = speed; l = long run; sn = scenic; tr = transcendental; gr = group run; adj = adjustment; fn = fun; fb = fat burning; nu = nutrition
mn = mental training; ag = afterglow; so = social

Monday

Goal	1	Comments
Run/Walk/Run strategy used:	2	
Time:	3	
Distance:	4	
AM Pulse:	5	
Weather:	6	
Temp:	7	
Time: AM PM	8	
Terrain:	9	
Date Walk Break:	10	

Tuesday

Goal	1	Comments
Run/Walk/Run strategy used:	2	
Time:	3	
Distance:	4	
AM Pulse:	5	
Weather:	6	
Temp:	7	
Time: AM PM	8	
Terrain:	9	
Date Walk Break:	10	

Wednesday

Goal	1	Comments
Run/Walk/Run strategy used:	2	
Time:	3	
Distance:	4	
AM Pulse:	5	
Weather:	6	
Temp:	7	
Time: AM PM	8	
Terrain:	9	
Date Walk Break:	10	

Thursday

Goal	1	Comments
Run/Walk/Run strategy used:	2	
Time:	3	
Distance:	4	
AM Pulse:	5	
Weather:	6	
Temp:	7	
Time: AM PM	8	
Terrain:	9	
Date Walk Break:	10	

Friday

Goal	1	Comments
Run/Walk/Run strategy used:	2	
Time:	3	
Distance:	4	
AM Pulse:	5	
Weather:	6	
Temp:	7	
Time: AM PM	8	
Terrain:	9	
Date Walk Break:	10	

Saturday

Goal	1	Comments
Run/Walk/Run strategy used:	2	
Time:	3	
Distance:	4	
AM Pulse:	5	
Weather:	6	
Temp:	7	
Time: AM PM	8	
Terrain:	9	
Date Walk Break:	10	

Sunday

Goal	1	Comments
Run/Walk/Run strategy used:	2	
Time:	3	
Distance:	4	
AM Pulse:	5	
Weather:	6	
Temp:	7	
Time: AM PM	8	
Terrain:	9	
Date Walk Break:	10	

Week of _____

HELP SOMEONE TO GET INTO RUNNING OR WALKING
AND YOU'LL RECEIVE A LOT MORE THAN YOU GIVE.

Sc = standard course; in = injury; sp = speed; l = long run; sn = scenic; tr = transcendental;
gr = group run; adj = adjustment; fn = fun; fb = fat burning; nu = nutrition
mn = mental training; ag = afterglow; so = social

Monday			Comments
Goal		1	
Run/Walk/Run strategy used:		2	
Time:		3	
Distance:		4	
AM Pulse:		5	
Weather:		6	
Temp:		7	
Time:	AM PM	8	
Terrain:		9	
Date	Walk Break:	10	

Tuesday			Comments
Goal		1	
Run/Walk/Run strategy used:		2	
Time:		3	
Distance:		4	
AM Pulse:		5	
Weather:		6	
Temp:		7	
Time:	AM PM	8	
Terrain:		9	
Date	Walk Break:	10	

Wednesday			Comments
Goal		1	
Run/Walk/Run strategy used:		2	
Time:		3	
Distance:		4	
AM Pulse:		5	
Weather:		6	
Temp:		7	
Time:	AM PM	8	
Terrain:		9	
Date	Walk Break:	10	

Thursday

Goal	1	Comments
Run/Walk/Run strategy used:	2	
Time:	3	
Distance:	4	
AM Pulse:	5	
Weather:	6	
Temp:	7	
Time: AM PM	8	
Terrain:	9	
Date Walk Break:	10	

Friday

Goal	1	Comments
Run/Walk/Run strategy used:	2	
Time:	3	
Distance:	4	
AM Pulse:	5	
Weather:	6	
Temp:	7	
Time: AM PM	8	
Terrain:	9	
Date Walk Break:	10	

Saturday

Goal	1	Comments
Run/Walk/Run strategy used:	2	
Time:	3	
Distance:	4	
AM Pulse:	5	
Weather:	6	
Temp:	7	
Time: AM PM	8	
Terrain:	9	
Date Walk Break:	10	

Sunday

Goal	1	Comments
Run/Walk/Run strategy used:	2	
Time:	3	
Distance:	4	
AM Pulse:	5	
Weather:	6	
Temp:	7	
Time: AM PM	8	
Terrain:	9	
Date Walk Break:	10	

Week of _____

AT THE FIRST SIGN OF A POSSIBLE INJURY, TAKE AN EXTRA ONE TO THREE DAYS OFF FROM RUNNING. THIS MAY HELP YOU AVOID A MONTH OR MORE OFF WHEN YOU PUSHED IT AND INCREASED THE DAMAGE.

Sc = standard course; in = injury; sp = speed; I = long run; sn = scenic; tr = transcendental; gr = group run; adj = adjustment; fn = fun; fb = fat burning; nu = nutrition
mn = mental training; ag = afterglow; so = social

Monday

Goal	1	Comments
Run/Walk/Run strategy used:	2	
Time:	3	
Distance:	4	
AM Pulse:	5	
Weather:	6	
Temp:	7	
Time: AM PM	8	
Terrain:	9	
Date Walk Break:	10	

Tuesday

Goal	1	Comments
Run/Walk/Run strategy used:	2	
Time:	3	
Distance:	4	
AM Pulse:	5	
Weather:	6	
Temp:	7	
Time: AM PM	8	
Terrain:	9	
Date Walk Break:	10	

Wednesday

Goal	1	Comments
Run/Walk/Run strategy used:	2	
Time:	3	
Distance:	4	
AM Pulse:	5	
Weather:	6	
Temp:	7	
Time: AM PM	8	
Terrain:	9	
Date Walk Break:	10	

Thursday

Goal	1	Comments
Run/Walk/Run strategy used:	2	
Time:	3	
Distance:	4	
AM Pulse:	5	
Weather:	6	
Temp:	7	
Time: AM/PM	8	
Terrain:	9	
Date Walk Break:	10	

Friday

Goal	1	Comments
Run/Walk/Run strategy used:	2	
Time:	3	
Distance:	4	
AM Pulse:	5	
Weather:	6	
Temp:	7	
Time: AM/PM	8	
Terrain:	9	
Date Walk Break:	10	

Saturday

Goal	1	Comments
Run/Walk/Run strategy used:	2	
Time:	3	
Distance:	4	
AM Pulse:	5	
Weather:	6	
Temp:	7	
Time: AM/PM	8	
Terrain:	9	
Date Walk Break:	10	

Sunday

Goal	1	Comments
Run/Walk/Run strategy used:	2	
Time:	3	
Distance:	4	
AM Pulse:	5	
Weather:	6	
Temp:	7	
Time: AM/PM	8	
Terrain:	9	
Date Walk Break:	10	

Week of _____

WE ARE DESIGNED TO RUN – AND WE INCREASE OUR CHANCE OF DAILY HAPPINESS WHEN WE DO SO.

Sc = standard course; in = injury; sp = speed; l = long run; sn = scenic; tr = transcendental; gr = group run; adj = adjustment; fn = fun; fb = fat burning; nu = nutrition mn = mental training; ag = afterglow; so = social

Monday

Goal	1	Comments
Run/Walk/Run strategy used:	2	
Time:	3	
Distance:	4	
AM Pulse:	5	
Weather:	6	
Temp:	7	
Time: AM PM	8	
Terrain:	9	
Date Walk Break:	10	

Tuesday

Goal	1	Comments
Run/Walk/Run strategy used:	2	
Time:	3	
Distance:	4	
AM Pulse:	5	
Weather:	6	
Temp:	7	
Time: AM PM	8	
Terrain:	9	
Date Walk Break:	10	

Wednesday

Goal	1	Comments
Run/Walk/Run strategy used:	2	
Time:	3	
Distance:	4	
AM Pulse:	5	
Weather:	6	
Temp:	7	
Time: AM PM	8	
Terrain:	9	
Date Walk Break:	10	

Thursday

Goal	1	Comments
Run/Walk/Run strategy used:	2	
Time:	3	
Distance:	4	
AM Pulse:	5	
Weather:	6	
Temp:	7	
Time: AM PM	8	
Terrain:	9	
Date Walk Break:	10	

Friday

Goal	1	Comments
Run/Walk/Run strategy used:	2	
Time:	3	
Distance:	4	
AM Pulse:	5	
Weather:	6	
Temp:	7	
Time: AM PM	8	
Terrain:	9	
Date Walk Break:	10	

Saturday

Goal	1	Comments
Run/Walk/Run strategy used:	2	
Time:	3	
Distance:	4	
AM Pulse:	5	
Weather:	6	
Temp:	7	
Time: AM PM	8	
Terrain:	9	
Date Walk Break:	10	

Sunday

Goal	1	Comments
Run/Walk/Run strategy used:	2	
Time:	3	
Distance:	4	
AM Pulse:	5	
Weather:	6	
Temp:	7	
Time: AM PM	8	
Terrain:	9	
Date Walk Break:	10	

Week of _____

YOU ONLY GET TO THE FINISH BECAUSE YOU KEPT PUSHING THROUGH THOSE MANY EPISODES WHEN THE LEFT BRAIN TOLD YOU TO QUIT.

Sc = standard course; **in** = injury; **sp** = speed; **l** = long run; **sn** = scenic; **tr** = transcendental; **gr** = group run; **adj** = adjustment; **fn** = fun; **fb** = fat burning; **nu** = nutrition **mn** = mental training; **ag** = afterglow; **so** = social

Monday

			Comments
Goal		1	
Run/Walk/Run strategy used:		2	
Time:		3	
Distance:		4	
AM Pulse:		5	
Weather:		6	
Temp:		7	
Time:	AM PM	8	
Terrain:		9	
Date Walk Break:		10	

Tuesday

			Comments
Goal		1	
Run/Walk/Run strategy used:		2	
Time:		3	
Distance:		4	
AM Pulse:		5	
Weather:		6	
Temp:		7	
Time:	AM PM	8	
Terrain:		9	
Date Walk Break:		10	

Wednesday

			Comments
Goal		1	
Run/Walk/Run strategy used:		2	
Time:		3	
Distance:		4	
AM Pulse:		5	
Weather:		6	
Temp:		7	
Time:	AM PM	8	
Terrain:		9	
Date Walk Break:		10	

Thursday

Goal		1	Comments	
Run/Walk/Run strategy used:		2		
Time:		3		
Distance:		4		
AM Pulse:		5		
Weather:		6		
Temp:		7		
Time:	AM PM	8		
Terrain:		9		
Walk Break:		10		

Date

Friday

Goal		1	Comments	
Run/Walk/Run strategy used:		2		
Time:		3		
Distance:		4		
AM Pulse:		5		
Weather:		6		
Temp:		7		
Time:	AM PM	8		
Terrain:		9		
Walk Break:		10		

Date

Saturday

Goal		1	Comments	
Run/Walk/Run strategy used:		2		
Time:		3		
Distance:		4		
AM Pulse:		5		
Weather:		6		
Temp:		7		
Time:	AM PM	8		
Terrain:		9		
Walk Break:		10		

Date

Sunday

Goal		1	Comments	
Run/Walk/Run strategy used:		2		
Time:		3		
Distance:		4		
AM Pulse:		5		
Weather:		6		
Temp:		7		
Time:	AM PM	8		
Terrain:		9		
Walk Break:		10		

Date

Week of _____

FEELING BETTER IS OFTEN AS SIMPLE AS RUNNNG (AND WALKING) DOWN THE ROAD, ABOUT ONE MILE.

Sc = standard course; in = injury; sp = speed; I = long run; sn = scenic; tr = transcendental; gr = group run; adj = adjustment; fn = fun; fb = fat burning; nu = nutrition
mn = mental training; ag = afterglow; so = social

Monday

Goal	1	Comments
Run/Walk/Run strategy used:	2	
Time:	3	
Distance:	4	
AM Pulse:	5	
Weather:	6	
Temp:	7	
Time: AM PM	8	
Terrain:	9	
Date Walk Break:	10	

Tuesday

Goal	1	Comments
Run/Walk/Run strategy used:	2	
Time:	3	
Distance:	4	
AM Pulse:	5	
Weather:	6	
Temp:	7	
Time: AM PM	8	
Terrain:	9	
Date Walk Break:	10	

Wednesday

Goal	1	Comments
Run/Walk/Run strategy used:	2	
Time:	3	
Distance:	4	
AM Pulse:	5	
Weather:	6	
Temp:	7	
Time: AM PM	8	
Terrain:	9	
Date Walk Break:	10	

Thursday

Goal	1	Comments
Run/Walk/Run strategy used:	2	
Time:	3	
Distance:	4	
AM Pulse:	5	
Weather:	6	
Temp:	7	
Time: AM PM	8	
Terrain:	9	
Walk Break:	10	

Date

Friday

Goal	1	Comments
Run/Walk/Run strategy used:	2	
Time:	3	
Distance:	4	
AM Pulse:	5	
Weather:	6	
Temp:	7	
Time: AM PM	8	
Terrain:	9	
Walk Break:	10	

Date

Saturday

Goal	1	Comments
Run/Walk/Run strategy used:	2	
Time:	3	
Distance:	4	
AM Pulse:	5	
Weather:	6	
Temp:	7	
Time: AM PM	8	
Terrain:	9	
Walk Break:	10	

Date

Sunday

Goal	1	Comments
Run/Walk/Run strategy used:	2	
Time:	3	
Distance:	4	
AM Pulse:	5	
Weather:	6	
Temp:	7	
Time: AM PM	8	
Terrain:	9	
Walk Break:	10	

Date

Week of _____

EACH TIME YOU PUSH THROUGH DOUBT AND FATIGUE, YOU'RE ACTIVATING THE INNER MECHANISM THAT MAKES IT EASIER TO DO IT AGAIN.

Sc = standard course; in = injury; sp = speed; l = long run; sn = scenic; tr = transcendental; gr = group run; adj = adjustment; fn = fun; fb = fat burning; nu = nutrition
mn = mental training; ag = afterglow; so = social

Monday

Goal	1	Comments
Run/Walk/Run strategy used:	2	
Time:	3	
Distance:	4	
AM Pulse:	5	
Weather:	6	
Temp:	7	
Time: AM PM	8	
Terrain:	9	
Date Walk Break:	10	

Tuesday

Goal	1	Comments
Run/Walk/Run strategy used:	2	
Time:	3	
Distance:	4	
AM Pulse:	5	
Weather:	6	
Temp:	7	
Time: AM PM	8	
Terrain:	9	
Date Walk Break:	10	

Wednesday

Goal	1	Comments
Run/Walk/Run strategy used:	2	
Time:	3	
Distance:	4	
AM Pulse:	5	
Weather:	6	
Temp:	7	
Time: AM PM	8	
Terrain:	9	
Date Walk Break:	10	

Thursday

Goal	1	Comments
Run/Walk/Run strategy used:	2	
Time:	3	
Distance:	4	
AM Pulse:	5	
Weather:	6	
Temp:	7	
Time: AM PM	8	
Terrain:	9	
Date Walk Break:	10	

Friday

Goal	1	Comments
Run/Walk/Run strategy used:	2	
Time:	3	
Distance:	4	
AM Pulse:	5	
Weather:	6	
Temp:	7	
Time: AM PM	8	
Terrain:	9	
Date Walk Break:	10	

Saturday

Goal	1	Comments
Run/Walk/Run strategy used:	2	
Time:	3	
Distance:	4	
AM Pulse:	5	
Weather:	6	
Temp:	7	
Time: AM PM	8	
Terrain:	9	
Date Walk Break:	10	

Sunday

Goal	1	Comments
Run/Walk/Run strategy used:	2	
Time:	3	
Distance:	4	
AM Pulse:	5	
Weather:	6	
Temp:	7	
Time: AM PM	8	
Terrain:	9	
Date Walk Break:	10	

Week of _____

EACH RUN HAS A SELF-FULFILLING REWARD: THE FINISH.

Monday

Goal	1	Comments
Run/Walk/Run strategy used:	2	
Time:	3	
Distance:	4	
AM Pulse:	5	
Weather:	6	
Temp:	7	
Time: AM PM	8	
Terrain:	9	
Date	Walk Break:	10	

Tuesday

Goal	1	Comments
Run/Walk/Run strategy used:	2	
Time:	3	
Distance:	4	
AM Pulse:	5	
Weather:	6	
Temp:	7	
Time: AM PM	8	
Terrain:	9	
Date	Walk Break:	10	

Wednesday

Goal	1	Comments
Run/Walk/Run strategy used:	2	
Time:	3	
Distance:	4	
AM Pulse:	5	
Weather:	6	
Temp:	7	
Time: AM PM	8	
Terrain:	9	
Date	Walk Break:	10	

Thursday

Goal	1	Comments
Run/Walk/Run strategy used:	2	
Time:	3	
Distance:	4	
AM Pulse:	5	
Weather:	6	
Temp:	7	
Time: AM PM	8	
Terrain:	9	
Date Walk Break:	10	

Friday

Goal	1	Comments
Run/Walk/Run strategy used:	2	
Time:	3	
Distance:	4	
AM Pulse:	5	
Weather:	6	
Temp:	7	
Time: AM PM	8	
Terrain:	9	
Date Walk Break:	10	

Saturday

Goal	1	Comments
Run/Walk/Run strategy used:	2	
Time:	3	
Distance:	4	
AM Pulse:	5	
Weather:	6	
Temp:	7	
Time: AM PM	8	
Terrain:	9	
Date Walk Break:	10	

Sunday

Goal	1	Comments
Run/Walk/Run strategy used:	2	
Time:	3	
Distance:	4	
AM Pulse:	5	
Weather:	6	
Temp:	7	
Time: AM PM	8	
Terrain:	9	
Date Walk Break:	10	

Week of _____

RUNNING IS A BALANCE OF PHYSICAL EXERTION, ENHANCED MENTAL AWARENESS AND SPIRITUAL PEACE.

Sc = standard course; in = injury; sp = speed; l = long run; sn = scenic; tr = transcendental; gr = group run; adj = adjustment; fn = fun; fb = fat burning; nu = nutrition mn = mental training; ag = afterglow; so = social

Monday

Goal		1	Comments
Run/Walk/Run strategy used:		2	
Time:		3	
Distance:		4	
AM Pulse:		5	
Weather:		6	
Temp:		7	
Time:	AM PM	8	
Terrain:		9	
Date	Walk Break:	10	

Tuesday

Goal		1	Comments
Run/Walk/Run strategy used:		2	
Time:		3	
Distance:		4	
AM Pulse:		5	
Weather:		6	
Temp:		7	
Time:	AM PM	8	
Terrain:		9	
Date	Walk Break:	10	

Wednesday

Goal		1	Comments
Run/Walk/Run strategy used:		2	
Time:		3	
Distance:		4	
AM Pulse:		5	
Weather:		6	
Temp:		7	
Time:	AM PM	8	
Terrain:		9	
Date	Walk Break:	10	

Thursday

			Comments
Goal		1	
Run/Walk/Run strategy used:		2	
Time:		3	
Distance:		4	
AM Pulse:		5	
Weather:		6	
Temp:		7	
Time:	AM PM	8	
Terrain:		9	
Date	Walk Break:	10	

Friday

			Comments
Goal		1	
Run/Walk/Run strategy used:		2	
Time:		3	
Distance:		4	
AM Pulse:		5	
Weather:		6	
Temp:		7	
Time:	AM PM	8	
Terrain:		9	
Date	Walk Break:	10	

Saturday

			Comments
Goal		1	
Run/Walk/Run strategy used:		2	
Time:		3	
Distance:		4	
AM Pulse:		5	
Weather:		6	
Temp:		7	
Time:	AM PM	8	
Terrain:		9	
Date	Walk Break:	10	

Sunday

			Comments
Goal		1	
Run/Walk/Run strategy used:		2	
Time:		3	
Distance:		4	
AM Pulse:		5	
Weather:		6	
Temp:		7	
Time:	AM PM	8	
Terrain:		9	
Date	Walk Break:	10	

Week of _____

SOMETIMES THE DIFFERENCE BETWEEN SUCCESS AND DISAPPOINTMENT IN RUNNING IS STARTING YOUR RUN 10 SECONDS PER MILE TOO FAST.

Sc = standard course; in = injury; sp = speed; I = long run; sn = scenic; tr = transcendental; gr = group run; adj = adjustment; fn = fun; fb = fat burning; nu = nutrition
mn = mental training; ag = afterglow; so = social

Monday

Goal	1	Comments
Run/Walk/Run strategy used:	2	
Time:	3	
Distance:	4	
AM Pulse:	5	
Weather:	6	
Temp:	7	
Time: AM PM	8	
Terrain:	9	
Date Walk Break:	10	

Tuesday

Goal	1	Comments
Run/Walk/Run strategy used:	2	
Time:	3	
Distance:	4	
AM Pulse:	5	
Weather:	6	
Temp:	7	
Time: AM PM	8	
Terrain:	9	
Date Walk Break:	10	

Wednesday

Goal	1	Comments
Run/Walk/Run strategy used:	2	
Time:	3	
Distance:	4	
AM Pulse:	5	
Weather:	6	
Temp:	7	
Time: AM PM	8	
Terrain:	9	
Date Walk Break:	10	

Thursday

Goal	1	Comments
Run/Walk/Run strategy used:	2	
Time:	3	
Distance:	4	
AM Pulse:	5	
Weather:	6	
Temp:	7	
Time: AM PM	8	
Terrain:	9	
Date Walk Break:	10	

Friday

Goal	1	Comments
Run/Walk/Run strategy used:	2	
Time:	3	
Distance:	4	
AM Pulse:	5	
Weather:	6	
Temp:	7	
Time: AM PM	8	
Terrain:	9	
Date Walk Break:	10	

Saturday

Goal	1	Comments
Run/Walk/Run strategy used:	2	
Time:	3	
Distance:	4	
AM Pulse:	5	
Weather:	6	
Temp:	7	
Time: AM PM	8	
Terrain:	9	
Date Walk Break:	10	

Sunday

Goal	1	Comments
Run/Walk/Run strategy used:	2	
Time:	3	
Distance:	4	
AM Pulse:	5	
Weather:	6	
Temp:	7	
Time: AM PM	8	
Terrain:	9	
Date Walk Break:	10	

Week of _____

DISTANCE RUNNING IS NOT A STRENGTH ACTIVITY – BUT ONE OF INERTIA. YOUR GOAL IS TO KEEP MOVING FORWARD IN THE MOST EFFICIENT WAY.

Sc = standard course; in = injury; sp = speed; l = long run; sn = scenic; tr = transcendental; gr = group run; adj = adjustment; fn = fun; fb = fat burning; nu = nutrition
mn = mental training; ag = afterglow; so = social

Monday

Goal	1	Comments
Run/Walk/Run strategy used:	2	
Time:	3	
Distance:	4	
AM Pulse:	5	
Weather:	6	
Temp:	7	
Time: _____ AM PM	8	
Terrain:	9	
Date — Walk Break:	10	

Tuesday

Goal	1	Comments
Run/Walk/Run strategy used:	2	
Time:	3	
Distance:	4	
AM Pulse:	5	
Weather:	6	
Temp:	7	
Time: _____ AM PM	8	
Terrain:	9	
Date — Walk Break:	10	

Wednesday

Goal	1	Comments
Run/Walk/Run strategy used:	2	
Time:	3	
Distance:	4	
AM Pulse:	5	
Weather:	6	
Temp:	7	
Time: _____ AM PM	8	
Terrain:	9	
Date — Walk Break:	10	

Thursday

Goal Run/Walk/Run strategy used:		Comments
Time:	3	
Distance:	4	
AM Pulse:	5	
Weather:	6	
Temp:	7	
Time: AM PM	8	
Terrain:	9	
Date Walk Break:	10	

(1, 2 in upper rows)

Friday

Goal Run/Walk/Run strategy used:		Comments
Time:	3	
Distance:	4	
AM Pulse:	5	
Weather:	6	
Temp:	7	
Time: AM PM	8	
Terrain:	9	
Date Walk Break:	10	

Saturday

Goal Run/Walk/Run strategy used:		Comments
Time:	3	
Distance:	4	
AM Pulse:	5	
Weather:	6	
Temp:	7	
Time: AM PM	8	
Terrain:	9	
Date Walk Break:	10	

Sunday

Goal Run/Walk/Run strategy used:		Comments
Time:	3	
Distance:	4	
AM Pulse:	5	
Weather:	6	
Temp:	7	
Time: AM PM	8	
Terrain:	9	
Date Walk Break:	10	

Week of _____

IF YOU HAVE A TIME GOAL IN A RACE OR SPEED WORKOUT, CONCENTRATE ON QUICKER TURNOVER OF THE FEET AND LEGS, NOT A LONGER STRIDE LENGTH.

Sc = standard course; in = injury; sp = speed; l = long run; sn = scenic; tr = transcendental; gr = group run; adj = adjustment; fn = fun; fb = fat burning; nu = nutrition mn = mental training; ag = afterglow; so = social

Monday

Goal	1	Comments
Run/Walk/Run strategy used:	2	
Time:	3	
Distance:	4	
AM Pulse:	5	
Weather:	6	
Temp:	7	
Time: AM PM	8	
Terrain:	9	
Date — Walk Break:	10	

Tuesday

Goal	1	Comments
Run/Walk/Run strategy used:	2	
Time:	3	
Distance:	4	
AM Pulse:	5	
Weather:	6	
Temp:	7	
Time: AM PM	8	
Terrain:	9	
Date — Walk Break:	10	

Wednesday

Goal	1	Comments
Run/Walk/Run strategy used:	2	
Time:	3	
Distance:	4	
AM Pulse:	5	
Weather:	6	
Temp:	7	
Time: AM PM	8	
Terrain:	9	
Date — Walk Break:	10	

Thursday

Goal	1	Comments
Run/Walk/Run strategy used:	2	
Time:	3	
Distance:	4	
AM Pulse:	5	
Weather:	6	
Temp:	7	
Time: AM PM	8	
Terrain:	9	
Date	Walk Break:	10

Friday

Goal	1	Comments
Run/Walk/Run strategy used:	2	
Time:	3	
Distance:	4	
AM Pulse:	5	
Weather:	6	
Temp:	7	
Time: AM PM	8	
Terrain:	9	
Date	Walk Break:	10

Saturday

Goal	1	Comments
Run/Walk/Run strategy used:	2	
Time:	3	
Distance:	4	
AM Pulse:	5	
Weather:	6	
Temp:	7	
Time: AM PM	8	
Terrain:	9	
Date	Walk Break:	10

Sunday

Goal	1	Comments
Run/Walk/Run strategy used:	2	
Time:	3	
Distance:	4	
AM Pulse:	5	
Weather:	6	
Temp:	7	
Time: AM PM	8	
Terrain:	9	
Date	Walk Break:	10

12 Form Improvement Drills – to Make Running Faster and Easier

The following drills have helped thousands of runners run more efficiently and faster. Each develops different capabilities, and each rewards the individual for running smoother, reducing impact, using momentum, and increasing the cadence or turnover of feet and legs. With each drill, you'll be teaching yourself to move more more directly and easily down the road.

When?

These should be done on a non-long run day. It is fine, however, to insert them into your warmup, before a race or a speed workout. Many runners have also told me that the drills are a nice way to break up an average run that otherwise might be called "boring."

CD – The Cadence Drill for faster turnover

This is an easy drill that helps you to become a smoother runner, using less effort. By doing it regularly, you pull all the elements of good running form together at the same time. One drill a week will help you step lightly, as you increase the number of steps per half minute. This will help you run faster, with less effort.

1. Warm up by walking for 5 minutes, and running and walking very gently for 10 minutes.

2. Start jogging slowly for 1-2 minutes, and then time yourself for 30 seconds. During this half minute, count the number of times your left foot touches the ground.

3. Walk around for a minute or so.

4. On the 2nd 30 second drill, increase the count by 1 or 2.

5. Repeat this 3-7 more times. Each time trying to increase by 1-2 additional counts.

In the process of improving turnover, the body's internal monitoring system, coordinates a series of adaptations which make the feet, legs, nerve system and timing mechanism work together as an efficient team:

- Your foot touches more gently

- Extra, inefficient motions of the foot and leg are reduced or eliminated

- Less effort is spent on pushing up or moving forward

- You stay lower to the ground

- The ankle does most of the work saving muscle resources

- Ache and pain areas are not overused

Acceleration-Glider Drills

This drill is a very easy and gentle form of speed play, or fartlek. By doing it regularly, you develop a range of speeds, with the muscle conditioning to move smoothly from one to the next. The greatest benefit comes as you learn how to "glide," or coast off your momentum.

1. Done on a non-long-run day, in the middle of a shorter run, or as a warmup for a speed session, a race or a magic mile.

2. Warm up with at least half a mile of easy running.

3. Many runners do the cadence drill just after the easy warmup, followed by the acceleration-gliders. But each can be done separately, if desired.

4. Run 4-8 of them.

5. Do this at least once a week.

6. No sprinting—never run all-out.

After teaching this drill at my one-day running schools and weekend retreats for years, I can say that most people learn better through practice when they work on the concepts listed below – rather than the details – of the drill. So just get out there and try them!

Gliding – The most important concept. This is like coasting off the momentum of a downhill run. You can do some of your gliders running down a hill if you want, but it is important to do at least two of them on the flat land.

Do this every week – As in the cadence drills, regularity is very important. If you're like most runners, you won't glide very far at first. Regular practice will help you glide farther and farther.

Don't sweat the small stuff – I've included a general guideline of how many steps to do with each part of the drill, but don't worry about getting any set number of steps. It's best to get into a flow with this drill and not worry about counting steps.

Smooth transition – between each of the components. Each time you "shift gears" you are using the momentum of the current mode to start you into the next mode. Don't make a sudden and abrupt change, but make a smooth transition between modes.

Here's how it's done:

- Start by jogging very slowly for about 15 steps.
- Then, jog faster for about 15 steps – increasing to a regular running pace for you.
- Now, over the next @ fifteen steps, gradually increase the speed to your current race pace.
- OK, it's time to glide, or coast. Allow yourself to gradually slow down to a jog using momentum as long as you can. At first you may only glide for 10-20 steps. As the months go by you will get up to 30 and beyond . . . you're gliding!

Overall Purpose: As you do this drill, every week, your form will become smoother at each mode of running. Congratulations! You are learning how to keep moving at a fairly fast pace without using much energy. This is the main object of the drill.

There will be some weeks when you will glide longer than others – don't worry about this. By doing this drill regularly, you will find yourself coasting or gliding down the smallest of inclines, and even for 10-20 yards on the flat, on a regular basis. Gliding conserves energy – reduces soreness, fatigue, and helps you maintain a faster pace in races.

13 A Standard Warm-up

How to warm up –
before races, race rehearsals, speedwork, MMs

1. Walk gently for three minutes

2. For 6-10 minutes, walk more than you would on an easy day: if you would normally run for 3 minutes/ walk for 1 minute, use a 1-1. If you normally run with 1-1 start with 15 seconds run/45 seconds walk or 20 sec run/40 sec walk.

3. Get into your usual run-walk-run strategy for 6-10 minutes

4. Do 4-8 acceleration-gliders. Gradually increase speed to that you will be running that day. No sprinting!

5. Walk for three minutes and start the workout, race, etc.

© iStockphoto/Thinkstock

14   Troubleshooting Performance

Times are slowing down at end

- Your long runs aren't long enough

- You are running too fast at the beginning of the race

- You may benefit from walk breaks that are taken more frequently

- You may be overtrained – put more rest between speed repetitions for a week or two

- In speed workouts, run easier in the first third and hardest at the end (but no sprinting)

- Temperature and/or humidity may be to blame – try slowing down from the beginning

  Note: usual slowdown in a marathon or long run is 30 sec/mi slower for every 5 degrees above 60F (20 sec/kilometer for every 2C above 14C)

Slowing down in the middle of the race

- You may be running too hard at the beginning – slow down by a few seconds each mile

- You may benefit from more frequent walk breaks

- In speedworkouts, work the hardest in the middle of the workout

Nauseous at the end

- You ran too fast at the beginning or the middle

- Temperature is above 65F/17C

- You ate too much (or drank too much) before the race or workout – even hours before

- You ate the wrong foods before the workout – most commonly, fat, fried foods, milk products, fibrous foods

Tired during workouts

- Low in B vitamins
- Low in iron – have a serum ferritin test, cook food in an iron skillet
- Not eating enough protein
- Blood sugar is low before exercise
- Not eating within 30 min of the finish of a run
- Eating too much fat – especially before or right after a run
- Running too many days per week
- Running too hard on long runs
- Running too hard on all running days
- Not taking enough walk breaks from the beginning of your runs
- Insufficient rest days between hard workouts

© Thomas Northcut/Photodisc/Thinkstock

15 Injury Troubleshooting – from One Runner to Another

Note: For more information see the book "Running Injuries", by Hannaford and Galloway, available at www.JeffGalloway.com

Quick Treatment Tips

For all injuries:

1. Take 3 days off from running or any activity that could aggravate the area

2. Avoid any activity that could aggravate the injury

3. As you return to running, stay below the threshold of further irritation with much more liberal walking

4. Don't stretch unless you have ilio-tibial band injury. Stretching keeps most injuries from healing.

Muscle injuries:

1. Call your doctor's office and see if you can take prescription strength anti inflammatory medication

2. See a sports massage therapist who has worked successfully on many runners

Tendon and foot injuries

1. Rub a chunk of ice directly on the area for 15 minutes every night (keep rubbing until the area gets numb—about 15 minutes)

Note: ice bags, or gel ice don't seem to do any good at all

2. Foot injuries sometimes are helped by a "boot" cast at first to start the healing process.

Knee injuries

1. Call your doctor's office to see if you can take prescription strength anti-inflammatory medication

2. See if you can do a little gentle walking, sometimes this helps

3. Sometimes the knee straps can relieve pain, ask your doctor, or experienced running store specialist

4. Get a shoe check to see if you are in the right shoe (if you over-pronate, a motion control shoe may help)

5. If you over-pronate, an orthotic may help.

6. If you have internal knee pain, glucosamine supplement, may help.

Knee pain

If you stop running at the first sign of a knee problem, it is common that it will go way after 3-5 days off. Try to pinpoint the causes. Make sure that your running courses don't have a slant or canter. Look at the most worn pair of shoes you have, even walking shoes. If there is wear on the inside of the forefoot, you probably overpronate. If you have repeat issues with knee pain, you may need a foot support or orthotic. Ask your doctor whether prescription-strength anti-inflammatory medication could help.

Outside of the knee pain – Iliotibial Band Syndrome

This band of fascia acts as a tendon, going down the outside of the leg from the hip to just below the knee. The pain is most commonly felt on the outside of the knee, but can be felt anywhere along the I-T band. I believe this to be a "wobble injury." When the running muscles get tired, the leg motion becomes sloppy. The I-T band tries to restrain the wobbling motion, but it cannot and gets overused. Once the healing has started (usually a few days off from running), most runners I've worked with tend to heal as fast when running gently as from a complete layoff. It is crucial to stay below the threshold of further irritation. Rolling with a foam roller has often moved the healing along at a faster pace.

Shin injuries

1. Rule out a stress fracture. In this case, the pain usually gets worse as you run – but check with your doctor. If it is a stress fracture, you must stop running for (usually) at least 8 weeks.

2. If the pain gradually goes away as you run on it, there is less worry of a stress fracture. This is probably a shin splint. By staying below the threshold of irritating the shin muscle, runners can generally run with shin splints. (check with doctor to be sure).

3. Take more walk breaks, run more slowly, etc.

- Inside pain – posterior shin splints. Irritation of the inside of the leg, coming up from the ankle is called "posterior tibial shin splints" and is often due to over pronation of the foot (foot rolls in at pushoff).

- Front of shin – anterior shin splints. When the pain is in the muscle on the front of the lower leg it is "anterior tibial shin splints." This is very often due to having too long a stride when running and especially when walking. Downhill terrain should be avoided as much as possible during the healing.

- Stress Fracture. If the pain is in a very specific place, and/or increases as you run, it could be a more serious problem: a stress fracture. This is unusual for beginning runners, but characteristic of those who do too much, too soon. It can also indicate low bone density. If you even suspect a stress fracture, do not run or do anything stressful on the leg and see a doctor. Stress fractures take weeks of no running, usually wearing a cast. There may also be a calcium deficiency.

Heel pain – Plantar Fascia

"The most effective treatment is putting your foot in a supportive shoe before supporting your body weight on the foot each morning."

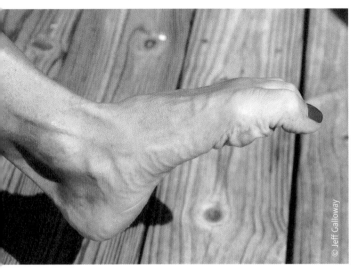

© Jeff Galloway

This very common injury (pain on the inside or center of the heel) is felt when taking the first few steps in the morning. As the foot moves and blood flow increases, the pain gradually goes away, only to return the next morning. Be sure to get a "shoe check" at a technical running store to make sure that you have the right shoe for your foot. If the pain is felt during the day, and is quite painful, you should consult with a podiatrist. Usually the doctor will construct a foot support that will surround your arch and heel. This does not always need to be a hard orthotic and is usually a softer one, at first, designed for your foot with build-ups in the right places.

The "toe squincher" exercise, can help develop foot strength that will also support the foot. It takes several weeks for this to take effect. The "squincher" is done by pointing your food down, and contracting the muscles in the foot similar to making a hard "fist" with your hand.

Back of the foot – Achilles Tendon

The achilles tendon is the narrow band of tendon rising up from the heel and connecting to the calf muscle. It is part of a very efficient mechanical system, and functions like a strong rubber band to leverage a lot of work out of the foot, with a little effort from the calf muscle. It is usually injured due to excessive stretching, either through running or through stretching exercises. First, avoid any activity that stretches the tendon in any way. It helps to add a small heel lift to all shoes, which reduces the range of motion. Every night, rub a chunk of ice directly on the tendon for about 15 minutes (until the tendon gets numb). Bags of ice or frozen gels don't do any good at all in my opinion. Usually after 3-5 days off from running, the icing takes hold and gets the injury in a healing mode. Anti-inflammatory medication very rarely helps with the achilles tendon, according to experts.

Hip and groin pain

There are a variety of elements that can result in aggravation in the hip area. Since the hips are not prime movers in running, they are usually abused when you continue to push on, when very fatigued. The hips try to do the work of the leg muscles and are not designed for this. Ask your doctor about prescription strength anti inflammatory medication, as this can often speed up recovery. Avoid stretching and any activity that aggravates the area.

Calf muscle pain

The calf is the most important muscle for running. It is often irritated by speedwork, and can be pushed into injury by stretching, running too fast when tired, speed sessions, inadequate rest between hard workouts, and sprinting at the end of races or workouts. Bouncing too high and running a lot of hills can also trigger this injury.

Deep tissue massage has been the best treatment for most calf muscle problems. Try to find a very experienced massage therapist who has helped lots of runners with calf problems. This treatment can be painful but is about the only way to remove some bio-damage in the muscle. The "stick" can move some of the damage out of the calf muscle (see our website for more information on this product).

Don't stretch! Stretching will tear the muscle fibers that are trying to heal. Avoid running hills or speed workouts, and take very frequent walk breaks as you return to running.

Re-starting your running before the injury has healed

Most of the runners I've worked with who have been injured, have been able to continue training while the injury is healing. But first, you must have some time off to get the healing started. If you do this at the beginning of an injury you may only need 2-5 days off. The longer you try to push through the problem, the greater the damage and the longer it will take to heal. Stay in touch with the doctor at any stage of this healing/running process, follow his/her advice, and use your best judgement.

To promote healing, once you have returned to running, stay below the threshold of further irritation. In other words, if the injury feels a little irritated when running at 2.5 miles, and starts hurting a little at 3 miles, you should run no more than 2 miles. And if your run-walk ratio is 4 min run/1 min walk, you should drop back to 2-1 or 1-1, or 30 seconds/30 seconds.

Take a day of rest between running days. With most injuries you can cross train to maintain conditioning, but make sure that your injury will allow this. Again, your doctor can advise.

Best cross training modes
to maintain your running conditioning

Before doing any of these ask your doctor. Most are fine for most injuries. But some run a risk of irritating the injured area and delaying the healing process. For more information on this, see the chapter on cross training, in my GALLOWAY'S BOOK ON RUNNING SECOND EDITION. Gradually increase the amount of cross training, because you have to condition those muscles gradually also. Walking is a great way to maintain conditioning if the injury and the doctor will allow it.

- Running in the water – can improve your running form
- Nordic Track machines
- Walking
- Rowing machines
- Eliptical machines

18

Training schedules:
5K, 10K,
Half Marathon,
Marathon

© John Foxx/Stockbyte/Thinkstock

5K – To Finish

Runners who are already running more than indicated can continue with their ratio of run-walk-run or continuous running.

Mon	Tue	Wed	Thu	Fri	Sat *	Sun
Week 1 (Walkers will walk only, runners will run for 15 seconds/walk for 45 seconds on the run/walk days)						
30 min run/walk	30 min walk	30 min run/walk	30 min walk	off	3 mi	off/walk
Week 2 (Walkers will walk only, runners will run for 15 seconds/walk for 45 seconds on the run/walk days)						
30 min run/walk	30 min walk	30 min run/walk	30 min walk	off	3.5 mi run/walk	off/walk
Week 3 (Walkers will walk only, runners will run for 20 seconds/walk for 40 seconds on the run/walk days)						
30 min run/walk	30 min walk	30 min run/walk	30 min walk	off	2 mi with MM	off/walk
Week 4 (Walkers will walk only, runners will run for 20 seconds/walk for 40 seconds on the run/walk days)						
30 min run/walk	30 min walk	30 min run/walk	30 min walk	off	4 mi run/walk	off/walk
Week 5 (Walkers will walk only, runners will run for 25 seconds/walk for 35 seconds on the run/walk days)						
30 min run/walk	30 min walk	30 min run/walk	30 min walk	off	2 mi with MM	off/walk
Week 6 (Walkers will walk only, runners will run for 25 seconds/walk for 35 seconds on the run/walk days)						
30 min run/walk	30 min walk	30 min run/walk	30 min walk	off	4.5 mi run/walk	off/walk
Week 7 (Walkers will walk only, runners will run for 30 seconds/walk for 30 seconds on the run/walk days)						
30 min run/walk	30 min walk	30 min run/walk	30 min walk	off	Goal Race	off/walk

* run the long run 4 min/mi slower than your magic mile predicts in the 5K, adjust for temperature
(MM = "magic mile" time trial, detailed on page 15)

10K – To Finish

Runners who are already running more than indicated can continue with their ratio of run-walk-run or continuous running.

Mon	Tue	Wed	Thu	Fri	Sat *	Sun
Week 1 (Walkers will walk only, runners will run for 15 seconds/walk for 45 seconds on the run/walk days)						
30 min run/walk	30 min walk	30 min run/walk	30 min walk	off	3 mi run/walk	off/walk
Week 2 (Walkers will walk only, runners will run for 15 seconds/walk for 45 seconds on the run/walk days)						
30 min run/walk	30 min walk	30 min run/walk	30 min walk	off	3.5 mi run/walk	off/walk
Week 3 (Walkers will walk only, runners will run for 15 seconds/walk for 45 seconds on the run/walk days)						
30 min run/walk	30 min walk	30 min run/walk	30 min walk	off	4 mi run/walk	off/walk
Week 4 (Walkers will walk only, runners will run for 20 seconds/walk for 40 seconds on the run/walk days)						
30 min run/walk	30 min walk	30 min run/walk	30 min walk	off	3 mi with MM	off/walk
Week 5 (Walkers will walk only, runners will run for 20 seconds/walk for 40 seconds on the run/walk days)						
30 min run/walk	30 min walk	30 min run/walk	30 min walk	off	4.5 mi run/walk	off/walk
Week 6 (Walkers will walk only, runners will run for 20 seconds/walk for 40 seconds on the run/walk days)						
30 min run/walk	30 min walk	30 min run/walk	30 min walk	off	5 mi run/walk	off/walk
Week 7 (Walkers will walk only, runners will run for 20 seconds/walk for 40 seconds on the run/walk days)						
30 min run/walk	30 min walk	30 min run/walk	30 min walk	off	3 mi with MM	off/walk

* run the long run 3.5 min/mi slower than your magic mile predicts in the 10K, adjust for temperature

(MM = "magic mile" time trial, detailed on page 15)

Mon	Tue	Wed	Thu	Fri	Sat *	Sun
Week 8 (Walkers will walk only, runners will run for 25 seconds/walk for 35 seconds on the run/walk days)						
30 min run/walk	30 min walk	30 min run/walk	30 min walk	off	5.5 mi run/walk	off/walk
Week 9 (Walkers, walk only, Runners will run for 25 seconds/walk for 35 seconds on the run/walk days)						
30 min run/walk	30 min walk	30 min run/walk	30 min walk	off	3 mi with MM	off/walk
Week 10 (Walkers, walk only. Runners will run for 25 seconds/walk for 35 seconds on the run/walk days)						
30 min run/walk	30 min walk	30 min run/walk	30 min walk	off	6 mi run/walk	off/walk
Week 11 (Walkers, walk only. Runners will run for 25 seconds/walk for 35 seconds on the run/walk days)						
30 min run/walk	30 min walk	30 min run/walk	30 min walk	off	3 mi with MM	off/walk
Week 12 (Walkers, walk only. Runners will run for 25 seconds/walk for 35 seconds on the run/walk days)						
30 min run/walk	30 min walk	30 min run/walk	30 min walk	off	6.5 mi run/walk	off/walk
Week 13 (Walkers, walk only. Runners will run for 30 seconds/walk for 30 seconds on the run/walk days)						
30 min run/walk	30 min walk	30 min run/walk	30 min walk	off	3 mi run/walk	off/walk
Week 14 (Walkers, walk only. Runners will run for 30 seconds/walk for 30 seconds on the run/walk days)						
30 min run/walk	30 min walk	30 min run/walk	30 min walk	off	Goal 10K	off/walk

Note: This training advice is given as one runner to another. For medical questions, ask your doctor.

For more training information, including time goal programs see my book 5K/10K which is available, autographed, at www.jeffgalloway.com

Half Marathon to finish

1. This program is designed for those who have already been running regularly, but have never run a half marathon before, or for veterans who don't have a time goal. To begin this program, you should have run a long run of at least 4 miles within the past two weeks. If your long run is not this long, then gradually increase the weekend run to this distance before beginning this program. If you have been running more than that listed on the schedule, it is usually OK to continue at that level.

2. What pace to run on the long runs? Read the section in this journal on pacing the long runs (page 15).

3. Run-walk-run ratio should correspond to the pace used (see page 20)

4. Pace for the half marathon itself: Run the first 10 miles (16K) at the training pace, noted above. If you want to speed up a little during the last 5K, go as you feel.

5. On long runs and the race itself, slow down when the temperature rises above 60F by 30 sec a mile for every 5 degrees above 60F or more (slow down 20 sec/KM for every 2C above 14C).

6. Tuesday and Thursday runs can be done at the pace of your choice.

7. It is fine to do cross training on Mon, Wed, and Fri. if you wish. There will be little benefit to your running in doing this, but you'll increase your fat burning. Don't do exercises like stair machines that use the calf muscle on days when you are resting from running.

8. Be sure to take a vacation from strenuous exercise, the day before your weekend runs.

9. An optional pace segment (p) is noted on the Thursday run. To get used to a pace you want to run in the race itself, time yourself for 1-3 miles, and take the walk breaks as you will do them in the race. This is especially important if you are anxious about finishing before the finish line is closed. This time is usually listed on the race website.

Week	Mon	Tue	Wed	Thu (p)	Fri	Sat	Sun *
1	off	30 min	off	30 min	easy walk	off	5 miles
2	off	30 min	off	30 min	easy walk	off	1 mi MM + 3 mi
3	off	30 min	off	30 min	easy walk	off	6,5 miles
4	off	30 min	off	30 min	easy walk	off	4 mile
5	off	30 min	off	30 min	easy walk	off	8 miles
6	off	30 min	off	30 min	easy walk	off	1 mi MM + 4 mi
7	off	30 min	off	30 min	easy walk	off	9,5 miles
8	off	30 min	off	30 min	easy walk	off	5 miles
9	off	30 min	off	30 min	easy walk	off	11 miles
10	off	30 min	off	30 min	easy walk	off	1 mi - MM + 4 mi
11	off	30 min	off	30 min	easy walk	off	12,5 miles
12	off	30 min	off	30 min	easy walk	off	5 miles
13	off	30 min	off	30 min	easy walk	off	14 miles
14	off	30 min	off	30 min	easy walk	off	1 mi MM + 4 mi
15	off	30 min	off	30 min	easy walk	off	**Half Marathon**
16	off	30 min	off	30 min	easy walk	off	3-5 miles

For time goal programs, see my book HALF MARATHON. This can be ordered, autographed, from www.jeffgalloway.com

Note: This training advice is given as one runner to another. For medical questions, ask your doctor.

* run the long run 3 min/mi slower than your magic mile predicts in the Half Marathon, adjust for temperature

(MM = "magic mile" time trial, detailed on page 15)

Marathon Training Schedule

To Finish

1. This program is designed for those who have already been running regularly, but have never run a marathon before, or for veterans who don't have a time goal. To begin this program, you should have run at long run of at least 3 miles (5K) within the past 2 weeks. If your long run is not this long, then gradually increase the weekend run to this distance. If you have been running more than what is listed on the schedule, it is usually OK to continue at that level.

2. What pace to run on the long runs? Read the section in this journal on pacing the long runs (page 15).

3. Run-walk-run ratio should correspond to the pace used (see page 20)

4. Pace for the marathon itself: Run the first 10 miles (16K) at the training pace, noted above. If you want to speed up a little during the last 5K, go as you feel.

5. On long runs and the race itself, slow down when the temperature rises above 60F by 30 seconds a mile for every 5 degrees above 60F or more (slow down 20 sec/KM for every 2C above 14C).

6. Tuesday and Thursday runs can be done at the pace of your choice.

7. It is fine to do cross training on Mon, Wed, and Fri. if you wish. There will be little benefit to your running in doing this, but you'll increase fat burning. Don't do exercises like stair machines that use the calf muscle on days when you are resting from running.

8. Be sure to take a vacation from strenuous exercise, the day before your long runs.

9. An optional pace segment (p) is noted on the Thursday run. To get used to a pace you want to run in the race itself, time yourself for 1-3 miles, and take the walk breaks as you will do them in the race. This is especially important if you are anxious about finishing before the finish line is closed. This time is usually listed on the race website.

Note: This training advice is given as one runner to another. For medical questions, ask your doctor.

For more training information, including time goal programs see my book Galloway's Marathon FAQs & A Year Round Plan which are available, autographed, at www.jeffgalloway.com

Week	Mon	Tue	Wed	Thu (p)	Fri	Sat	Sun *
1	off	30 min	off	30 min	easy walk	off	3 miles
2	off	30 min	off	30 min	easy walk	off	1 mi MM + 2 mi
3	off	30 min	off	30 min	easy walk	off	4 miles
4	off	30 min	off	30 min	easy walk	off	3 miles
5	off	30 min	off	30 min	easy walk	off	5 miles
6	off	30 min	off	30 min	easy walk	off	3 miles
7	off	30 min	off	30 min	easy walk	off	6,5 miles
8	off	30 min	off	30 min	easy walk	off	3 miles
9	off	30 min	off	30 min	easy walk	off	8 miles
10	off	30 min	off	30 min	easy walk	off	3 miles
11	off	30 min	off	30 min	easy walk	off	9,5 miles
12	off	30 min	off	30 min	easy walk	off	3 miles
13	off	30 min	off	30 min	easy walk	off	11 miles
14	off	30 min	off	30 min	easy walk	off	3 miles
15	off	30 min	off	30 min	easy walk	off	13 miles
16	off	30 min	off	30 min	easy walk	off	3 miles with MM
17	off	30 min	off	30 min	easy walk	off	15 miles
18	off	30 min	off	30 min	easy walk	off	3 miles with MM
19	off	30 min	off	30 min	easy walk	off	17 miles
20	off	30 min	off	30 min	easy walk	off	6 miles
21	off	30 min	off	30 min	easy walk	off	6 miles with MM
22	off	30 min	off	30 min	easy walk	off	20 miles
23	off	30 min	off	30 min	easy walk	off	6 miles
24	off	30 min	off	30 min	easy walk	off	6 miles with MM
25	off	30 min	off	30 min	easy walk	off	23 miles
26	off	30 min	off	30 min	easy walk	off	6 miles
27	off	30 min	off	30 min	easy walk	off	6 miles with MM
28	off	30 min	off	30 min	easy walk	off	26 miles
29	off	30 min	off	30 min	easy walk	off	6 miles
30	off	30 min	off	30 min	easy walk	off	6 miles
31	off	30 min	off	30 min	easy walk	off	**Marathon**
32	off	30 min	off	30 min	easy walk	off	3-5 miles

* run the long run 2 min/mi slower than your magic mile predicts in the Marathon, adjust for temperature

 (MM = "magic mile" time trial, detailed on page 15)

My Prediction for this Year

Date	Prediction	Actual

Predicting Race Performance

5KTime	Marathon	Half Marathon	5KTime	Marathon	Half Marathon
13:20	2:10:00	1:01:24	16:08	2:38:44	1:14:45
13:25	2:10:46	1:01:45	16:15	2:39:53	1:15:17
13:29	2:11:32	1:02:06	16:22	2:41:02	1:15:49
13:34	2:12:19	1:02:28	16:29	2:42:13	1:16:22
13:38	2:13:06	1:02:50	16:36	2:43:24	1:16:54
13:43	2:13:54	1:03:13	16:43	2:44:37	1:17:28
13:48	2:14:43	1:03:35	16:50	2:45:50	1:18:03
13:53	2:15:32	1:03:58	16:57	2:47:05	1:18:37
13:58	2:16:22	1:04:22	17:04	2:48:21	1:19:12
14:03	2:17:12	1:04:46	17:12	2:49:38	1:19:48
14:08	2:18:04	1:05:09	17:19	2:50:56	1:20:24
14:13	2:18:55	1:05:33	17:27	2:52:15	1:21:01
14:18	2:19:48	1:05:57	17:35	2:53:36	1:21:38
14:23	2:20:41	1:06:22	17:43	2:54:58	1:22:16
14:28	2:21:34	1:06:47	17:51	2:56:21	1:22:54
14:34	2:22:29	1:07:13	17:59	2:57:45	1:23:33
14:39	2:23:24	1:07:38	18:07	2:59:11	1:24:13
14:44	2:24:20	1:08:04	18:15	3:00:39	1:24:53
14:50	2:25:16	1:08:30	18:24	3:02:07	1:25:34
14:56	2:26:13	1:08:57	18:32	3:03:37	1:26:16
15:01	2:27:11	1:09:24	18:41	3:05:09	1:26:58
15:07	2:28:10	1:09:51	18:50	3:06:42	1:27:41
15:13	2:29:10	1:10:18	18:59	3:08:17	1:28:24
15:19	2:30:10	1:10:47	19:08	3:09:53	1:29:09
15:25	2:31:11	1:11:15	19:18	3:11:32	1:29:54
15:31	2:32:13	1:11:44	19:27	3:13:11	1:30:40
15:37	2:33:16	1:12:13	19:37	3:14:53	1:31:27
15:43	2:34:20	1:12:42	19:47	3:16:36	1:32:14
15:49	2:35:25	1:13:13	19:57	3:18:21	1:33:02
15:55	2:36:30	1:13:43	20:07	3:20:08	1:33:52
16:02	2:37:37	1:14:14	20:17	3:21:57	1:34:42

5KTime	Marathon	Half Marathon	5KTime	Marathon	Half Marathon
20:27	3:23:48	1:35:33	27:55	4:44:36	2:12:22
20:38	3:25:41	1:36:25	28:15	4:48:17	2:14:02
20:49	3:27:36	1:37:18	28:35	4:52:04	2:15:44
21:00	3:29:34	1:38:11	28:56	4:55:57	2:17:29
21:11	3:31:33	1:39:07	29:18	4:59:56	2:19:18
21:23	3:33:35	1:40:02	29:39	5:04:02	2:21:08
21:34	3:35:39	1:40:59	30:02	5:08:15	2:23:01
21:46	3:37:46	1:41:57	30:25	5:12:34	2:24:59
21:58	3:39:55	1:42:56	30:49	5:17:01	2:26:59
22:10	3:42:06	1:43:57	31:13	5:21:36	2:29:01
22:23	3:44:21	1:44:57	31:38	5:26:19	2:31:08
22:36	3:46:38	1:46:00	32:05	5:31:12	2:33:30
22:49	3:48:58	1:47:05	32:31	5:36:17	2:36:00
23:02	3:51:21	1:48:10	32:59	5:41:23	2:38:30
23:16	3:53:46	1:49:17	33:28	5:46:50	2:41:00
23:30	3:56:15	1:50:24	33:55	5:51:58	2:43:30
23:44	3:58:47	1:51:33	34:19	5:56:01	2:46:00
23:58	4:01:23	1:52:45	34:48	6:01:24	2:48:00
24:13	4:04:02	1:53:57	35:05	6:05:00	2:49:00
24:28	4:06:44	1:55:11	35:30	6:10:00	2:51:00
24:43	4:09:30	1:56:26	35:55	6:15:00	2:53:00
24:59	4:12:20	1:57:44	36:20	6:20:00	2:55:00
25:15	4:15:13	1:59:03	36:45	6:25:00	2:57:00
25:31	4:18:11	2:00:24	37:10	6:30:00	2:59:00
25:47	4:21:13	2:01:47	37:35	6:35:00	3:01:00
26:04	4:24:19	2:03:11	38:00	6:40:00	3:03:00
26:22	4:27:29	2:04:37	38:25	6:45:00	3:05:00
26:40	4:30:45	2:06:06	38:50	6:50:00	3:07:00
26:58	4:34:05	2:07:36	39:15	6:55:00	3:09:00
27:16	4:37:30	2:09:09	39:45	7:00:00	3:11:00
27:35	4:41:00	2:10:44			

AM Pulse Graph

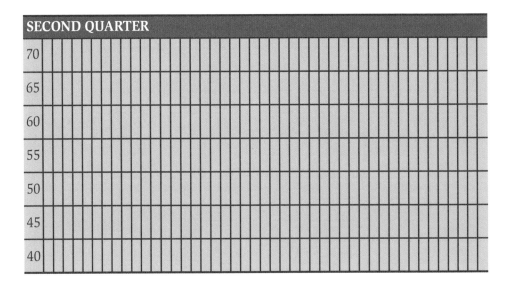

Note: Make sure that you take your pulse as soon as you are conscious, before your thoughts or motions increase the heart rate. If you can do this automatically, this graph will give you one of the best readings of overtraining. After several months of recording, you'll establish a "normal low." When the level rises more than five percent about this, take it easy. If pulse is more than 10 percent above, take the day off.

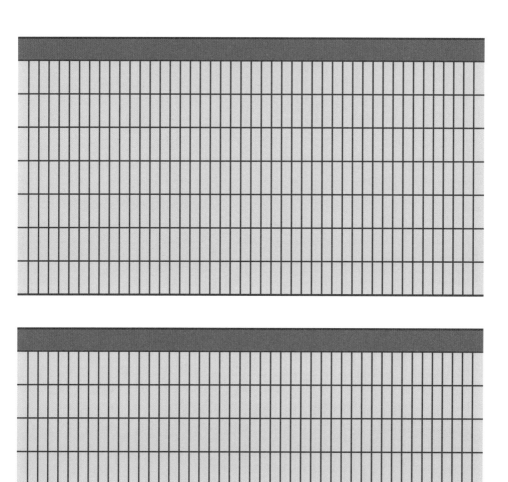

THIRD QUARTER

70
65
60
55
50
45
40

FOURTH QUARTER

70
65
60
55
50
45
40

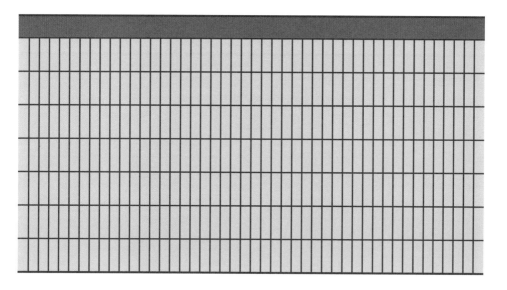

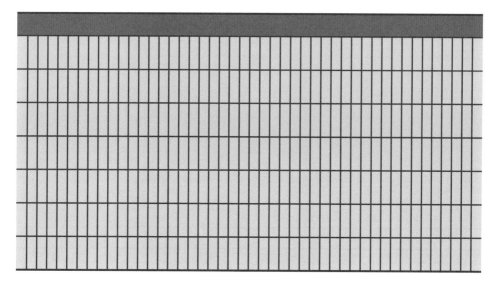

Injury Log

from running (walk, cross-train, etc.)

Injury:

First Noticed: When lost function:

Symptoms:

Treatment:

What I learnd:

Injury:

First Noticed: When lost function:

Symptoms:

Treatment:

What I learnd:

Injury:

First Noticed: When lost function:

Symptoms:

Treatment:

Injury:

First Noticed: When lost function:

Symptoms:

Treatment:

What I learnd:

Injury:

First Noticed: When lost function:

Symptoms:

Treatment:

What I learnd:

Injury:

First Noticed: When lost function:

Symptoms:

Treatment:

What I learnd:

Race Log

Be sure to paste in your proofs from race photo mailings.

Date	Race	Time	Weather

Comments:

Date	Race	Time	Weather

Comments:

Date	Race	Time	Weather

Comments:

Date	Race	Time	Weather

Comments:

Date	Race	Time	Weather

Comments:

Date	Race	Time	Weather

Comments:

Date	Race	Time	Weather

Comments:

Date	Race	Time	Weather

Comments:

Speed Sessions

Date	Goal	Session W/times	Comments

Date	Goal	Session W/times	Comments

Shoe Log

Date purchased	Brand model	Size	Date replaced	Mileage total	Comments

This year's Successes:

Success	What's next

Mistakes I've made this year:

_____

_____

_____

_____

_____

_____

_____

_____

_____

_____

_____

_____

_____

_____

_____

_____

_____

_____

_____

_____

_____

_____

_____

_____

YOUR PERSONAL RUNNING COACH

ISBN: 978184263335
E-Book: 9781841267241
$ 16.95 US/$ 29.95 AUS
£ 12.95 UK/€ 16.95

ISBN: 9781841262840
E-Book: 9781841265285
$ 16.95 US/$ 29.95 AUS
£ 12.95 UK/€ 16.95

ISBN: 9781841262918
E-Book: 9781841266992
$ 18.95 US/$ 32.95 AUS
£ 14.95 UK/€ 18.95

ISBN: 9781841263151
E-Book: 9781841267166
$ 18.95 US/$ 32.95 AUS
£ 14.95 UK/€ 18.95

All books available as mediaTresor E-books.
Secure & user-friendly

Fore more books by Jeff Galloway visit:

■ online
www.m-m-sports.com

■ E-Mail
sales@m-m-sports.com

MEYER
& MEYER
SPORT